OMAGH COLLEG

CX00018395

D1614998

KEY PAPERS ON
COUNTERTRANSFERENCE

IJP EDUCATION SECTION

Bo   to be   fore

W

KEY PAPERS ON COUNTERTRANSFERENCE

IJP EDUCATION SECTION

edited by
Robert Michels
Liliane Abensour
Claudio Laks Eizirik
Richard Rusbridger

International Journal of Psychoanalysis Key Papers Series
Series Editors: Paul Williams and Glen O. Gabbard

LONDON   NEW YORK

First published in 2002 by
H. Karnac (Books) Ltd.
6 Pembroke Buildings,
London NW10 6RE

Arrangement, Introduction © 2002 Institute of Psychoanalysis; chapters 2–5
copyright © 2002 Institute of Psychoanalysis, republished by
permission of the *International Journal of Psychoanalysis*.

The rights of the authors of this work
have been asserted in accordance with §§ 77 and 78 of the
Copyright Design and Patents Act 1988.

All rights reserved. No part of this publication may be reproduced, stored in
a retrieval system, or transmitted, in any form or by any means, electronic,
mechanical, photocopying, recording, or otherwise, without the prior written
permission of the publisher.

British Library Cataloguing in Publication Data

A C.I.P. for this book is available from the British Library

ISBN 1 85575 961 6

Produced for Karnac Books Ltd by
The Studio Publishing Services Ltd, 4A Brookside Units, Venny Bridge, Exeter
EX4 8JN

www.karnacbooks.com

CONTENTS

The International Journal of Psychoanalysis Key Papers Series

This series brings together the most important psychoanalytic papers in the *Journal*'s eighty-year history, in a series of accessible monographs. The idea behind the series is to approach the *IJP*'s intellectual resource from a variety of perspectives in order to highlight important domains of psychoanalytic enquiry. It is hoped that these volumes will be of interest to psychoanalysts, students of the discipline and, in particular, to those who work and write from an interdisciplinary standpoint. The ways in which the papers in the monographs are grouped will vary: for example, a number of 'themed' monographs will take as their subject important psychoanalytic topics, while others will stress interdisciplinary links (between neuroscience, anthropology, philosophy etc. and psychoanalysis). Still others will contain review essays on, for example, film and psychoanalysis, art and psychoanalysis and the worldwide *IJP* Internet Discussion Group, which debates important papers before they appear in the printed journal (cf. www.ijpa.org). The aim of all the monographs is to provide the reader with a substantive contribution of the highest quality that reflects the principal concerns of contemporary psychoanalysts and those with whom they are in dialogue. We hope you will find the monographs rewarding and pleasurable to read.

Paul Williams and Glen O. Gabbard
Joint Editors-in-Chief,
International Journal of Psychoanalysis
London, 2002

Introduction

RICHARD RUSBRIDGER

It often happens in psychoanalysis that phenomena which are first described as abnormal are later seen to occur more generally and normally. This is true of psychoanalysis as a theory of mind and of development, as seen in the case of the Oedipus complex, which Freud first described as pathological and later as universal and normal. It is also true of psychoanalysis as a psychotherapy, as in the case of the transference. This was initially seen by Freud as an impediment to therapeutic progress; later as one of the main means of making therapeutic progress; and finally as a universal theme of all relationships. Freud's notion of the transference also broadened in that he changed from seeing it as manifested in particular transferences as they came up in sessions—as in his treatment of Dora (Freud, 1905 [1901]) or of the Rat Man (Freud, 1909)—to seeing the transference more widely as a repetition in the therapy of all the patient's characteristic infantile conflicts.

Psychoanalysis is both a study of psychic pathology and, derived from that, an account of normal psychology. The move from seeing a phenomenon as pathology to describing it in normality is nowhere as marked as with the notion of counter-transference. Freud used it—first in a letter to Jung in 1909 (Freud &

Jung, 1974), and then in his address to the Nuremberg Congress the following year (Freud, 1910)—to refer to what he saw as the pathological and unhelpful stirring up in the analyst of unanalysed and potentially disruptive impulses. These were the counterpart in the analyst of the patient's resistance as expressed in the transference. Probably influenced by his turmoil over Jung's affair at this time with a patient [see Freud's extensive correspondence with Jung 1906–1909 (Freud & Jung, 1974)], he said that it constituted a "permanent problem for us" and needed to be "dominated" by what he called a "thick skin" (Freud, 1910). The papers in this volume were commissioned with a view to describing the current views of countertransference, and their historical evolution, in four intellectual communities of psychoanalysis: North America, Britain, France and Latin America. Psychoanalysis nowadays has a plurality of schools, and the idea of countertransference has been developed differently in these various arenas.

The papers in this book describe the radical, if uneven, development from this view to the point where the analyst's countertransference feelings for his patient (in the widened sense of his total emotional response to the patient, unconscious, preconscious and conscious) are seen as some of the most crucial data available to him or her. This change seems to have been developing in a number of different parts of the world simultaneously during the 1940s, and to have been described in the years around 1950 (Winnicott, 1949; Heimann, 1950; Little, 1951; Racker, 1953 [1948]). Some writers, influenced by Bion's (1959) model of the containment of anxiety, go further and see in the analyst's work of reflection on his or her countertransference and its inevitable enactment as being the mutative activity in analysis, preceding and informing the interpretation of transference (see, for example, Pick, 1985; Carpy, 1989).

This move is, however, not as simple as this makes it appear. On the one hand, right from the start of psychoanalysis the feelings aroused in the analyst by the patient have also been seen as crucial to the analyst's understanding. In three famous passages (1913, p. 320; 1915, p. 194; and 1923 [1922], p. 239) Freud writes about his fascination with the ways in which one unconscious can communicate with another person's unconscious directly—the very area that later writers subsumed under the term "countertransference".

And on the other hand, the later widening and development of the concept is accompanied by repeated cautions about the dangers of its misuse (Reich, 1951; Lacan, 1960). Lacan feared that the analytic situation, which he saw as, crucially, asymmetrical as between the roles of the analyst and patient, might be reduced to symmetry if the analyst's countertransference was seen as no more than the equivalent of the patient's transference. Klein warned that the analyst must not naïvely equate his or her feelings in the countertransference with the patient's feelings, or use the notion of countertransference to excuse his or her technical mistakes (Spillius, 1992, p. 62).

Most later writings on countertransference referred to in this volume are impressed by the powerfulness of the impact of the countertransference on the analyst (M'Uzan, 1978, describes it as being like the "mouth of the unconscious"). However, for that very reason they stress how crucial it is for the analyst to subject his or her feelings to careful scrutiny once he or she becomes aware of them. Unscrutinized, they can lead to an impasse and to enactments which persist rather than being used in the service of under- standing. An extreme degree of the patient's influence on the analyst's feelings was described by Grinberg (1956) as projective counter-identification. He described the patient having a fantasy of putting parts of his self, through projective identification, into the analyst's mind. The analyst then identifies himself with such parts and acts them out, becoming unable to understand the process or to function as a container, thereby becoming controlled by the patient. Grinberg described this as happening mainly with patients with severe personality disorders. If the analyst can recognize the disturbance of his or her feelings (of, say, irritation, erotic arousal or boredom) and detach himself or herself from them so as to reflect on them, they can be used as data, particularly about affects of which the patient may not yet be consciously aware, or which he or she cannot yet put into words. If the analyst can find a way of using these feelings to construct an interpretation, then what was previously unable to be thought can become known (Bollas, 1987). This essential, mutative, step is described by writers as distinct as the Barangers— who describe it (1983) as "taking a second look"—and Bion (1959). It is the same process as referred to by Britton (1989) as achieving triangular psychic space, the capacity to adopt a third position, in identification with the Oedipal parent of the same sex.

Countertransference, then, provokes both anxiety together with exhortations about its dangers; and enthusiasm and appeals for its centrality to be recognized. One way of understanding this enduring polarity is perhaps to appreciate that as most of the countertransference is unconscious it inevitably produces anxiety, dread and avoidance as well as fascination. Another is suggested by Chasseguet-Smirgel (1984) in a paper about the sexual identifications of the analyst in the course of his or her work. She makes the point that much analytic work involves the analyst in adopting a maternal, receptive, role, and that some analysts are not at ease with the female identification that this entails. This would perhaps apply pre-eminently to the analyst's attitude of receptivity to the feelings projected by or evoked by the patient. Chasseguet-Smirgel implies that analysts who find this aspect of the work difficult may tend to give preference to those aspects of the work which involve more penetrative, masculine identifications. It is then perhaps not surprising to find analysts tending to stress one role at the expense of the other.

Jacobs describes the scene in North America, but begins his paper with a discussion of the development of the idea of counter-transference before the explosion of interest in the topic around 1950. He mentions in particular the role of Ferenczi, Deutsch, Strachey and Low. He emphasizes the effect, already described, of Reich in inhibiting discussion of the topic in the fifties and sixties; and the relatively later development in the States of discussion of counter-transference than in other regions. Jacobs describes how, stimulated in particular by Kohut, there has been a flood of papers in the States about countertransference from the 1970s onwards. He discusses in particular the thinking of Ogden and Renik.

Hinshelwood describes the situation in Britain, particularly noting the Kleinian and post-Kleinian development of the notion of countertransference. He dissects out the significant differences in the use of the idea among Kleinian analysts, those more influenced by the work of Winnicott, and the "Contemporary Freudians" such as Sandler. Like the other authors, he makes a comparison between how the idea of countertransference has developed in his own intellectual/geographical arena and how it has developed else-where in the world.

Duparc starts by describing the effects of Lacan's thinking in inhibiting the development of thinking about countertransference in France, before also describing the many developments in the area from the 1970s onwards. Authors whom he describes as having made a significant contribution include Viderman, Neyraut, Aulagnier, M'Uzan, McDougall and Donnet. Duparc then summarizes his own views on the topic, stressing the way in which unmanageable and as yet unconceptualized difficulties of the patient can make themselves known in the first place in the form of countertransference experiences, often disturbing, in the analyst. In this he has much in common with Bollas (1987).

Bernardi's account of the Latin American scene starts with Racker and the Barangers, before describing the inhibiting effect of Lacan in South America as in France on the discussion of countertransference. She pays particular attention to the Barangers' concept of the *baluarte*, or bulwark, in the countertransference, a particular form of resistance shared by the patient and the analyst which gives rise to analytic impasses, and which necessitates careful self-examination (the "second look") on the part of the analyst.

Psychoanalysis is still sometimes described as a monolithic and unchanging theory and practice. These papers vividly contradict such a view through their close study of the evolution of the concept of countertransference from the periphery of psychoanalysis to its current position of central importance in most analytic communities. In doing so, they provide a window on the development of a living and evolving discipline during its first hundred years.

References

Baranger, W. *et al*. (1983). Cambios de la interpretación en el psicoanálisis del Uruguay entre 1960 y 1990. *Rev. Uruguaya Piscoanál.*, *84/85*: 89–102.

Bion, W. R. (1959). Attacks on linking. *Int. J. Psychoanal.*, 40: 308–315. In: *Second Thoughts*. London: Heinemann, 1967, and reprinted London: Karnac Books, 1984

Bollas, C. (1987). *The Shadow of the Object: Psychoanalysis of the Unthought Known*. London: Routledge.

Britton, R. (1989). The missing link: parental sexuality in the Oedipus Complex. In: J. Steiner (Ed.), *The Oedipus Complex Today*. London: Karnac Books.

Carpy, D. (1989). Tolerating the countertransference: a mutative process. *Int. J. Psycho-Anal.*, 70: 287–294.

Chasseguet-Smirgel, J. (1984). The femininity of the analyst in professional practice. *Int. J. Psycho-Anal.*, 65: 169–178.

Freud, S, (1905) [1901]) *Fragment of an Analysis of a Case of Hysteria. S.E.*, 7: 3–122.

Freud, S. (1909). Notes upon a case of obsessional neurosis. *S.E.*, 10.

Freud, S. (1910). The future prospects of psycho-analytic therapy. *S.E.*, 10: 141–151.

Freud, S. (1913). The disposition to obsessional neurosis. *S.E.*, 12: 313–326.

Freud, S. (1915). The Unconscious. *S.E.*, 14: 161–215.

Freud, S. (1923 [1922]). Two encyclopaedia articles. *S.E.*, 18.

Freud, S., & Jung, C. G. (1974). W. McGuire (Ed.), *The Freud/Jung Letters*. Princeton, NJ: Princeton University Press.

Grinberg, L. (1956). Sobre algunos problemas de técnica psicoanalítica determinados por la identificación y contraidentificación proyectivas. *Rev. Psychoanál.*, 13: 507–11.

Heimann, P. (1950). On countertransference. *Int. J. Psychoanal.*, 31: 81–84.

Lacan, J. (1960). *L'éthique de la Psychanalyse, Séminaire No 7*. Paris: Seuil. Published in English as *The Seminars of Jacques Lacan, Book VII*, D. Porter (Trans.). New York: Norton, 1992.

Little, M. (1951). Countertransference and the patient's response to it. *Int. J. Psychoanal.*, 32: 32–40.

M'Uzan, M. de (1978). La bouche de l'inconscient. In: *La Bouche de l'Inconscient*. Paris: Gallimard, 1994.

Pick, I. B. (1985). Working through in the countertransference. *Int. J. Psycho-Anal.*, 66: 157

Racker, H. (1953 [1948]). A contribution to the problem of counter-transference. *Int. J. Psycho-Anal.*, 34: 313–24. First given to the Argentine Psychoanalytic Association, 1948, as "La neurosis de contratransferencia".

Reich, A. (1951). On countertransference. *Int. J. Psychoanal.*, 32: 25–31.

Spillius, E. B. (1992). Clinical experiences of projective identification. In: R. Anderson (Ed.), *Clinical Lectures on Klein and Bion* (pp. 59–73). London: Routledge.

Winnicott, D. W. (1949). Hate in the countertransference. *Int. J. Psychoanal.*, 30: 69–75.

1: Countertransference past and present: a review of the concept

THEODORE J. JACOBS, New York

My purpose in this paper is to review the major trends and developments in the evolution of the concept of countertransference. I will do so from my own perspective; that is, from the viewpoint of one American analyst, trained in a classical institute, who has had a long-standing interest in this issue.

Although I will attempt to describe some of the questions and controversies that have surrounded the idea of countertransference as well as the viewpoints of many of those who have written on the subject, I will make no attempt to be all-inclusive. My effort, rather, will be to present an overview of a concept, long in the shadows, that has emerged as one of the issues most actively discussed and debated in psychoanalysis today.

Looking back on the final decades of the twentieth century, in fact, future historians of psychoanalysis may well designate this period the countertransference years; for in this time few concepts in our field have gained as much attention, have been as widely explored and written about, and have been the subject of as much controversy as has the question of countertransference and its role in the analytic process. Certainly in America, but also, to a considerable extent worldwide, countertransference and the closely related issues of intersubjectivity, enactments, self-analysis and the question of neutrality have taken centre stage as matters with which contemporary analysts are much preoccupied.

One could say, then, of countertransference, that it is a concept whose time has come; or perhaps more accurately, that it is a concept that, like the proverbial groundhog, has emerged into the sunlight when the conditions were right after having previously poked its head into the air, tested the weather, and retreated below ground. The creature who has now appeared, however, is essentially the same one who did the initial reconnoitring; more sprightly and energetic, perhaps, but basically unchanged. What has prompted his re-emergence is not some fundamental alteration in himself. It is a change in the climate, a change in the analytic atmosphere that has made it possible for the familiar face of countertransference to reappear.

A review of the literature on the concept, in other words, makes clear that although relatively little was written about counter-transference in the first half of this century, those authors who were interested in the topic raised many of the issues that, today, are being actively discussed and debated in our psychoanalytic societies. The time was not right, however, for a full exploration of the topic of countertransference. It took a change in the intellectual climate, both within and outside of analysis; and, in America, a change in the analytic establishment for this to happen.

Writers on countertransference have pointed out that although he was the first to identify and describe the phenomenon, Freud actually had little more to say about it. In fact, while it is true that Freud's comments on countertransference were sparse, what he did say, I believe, is of the greatest importance. His brief remarks on the topic have served as the source and foundation for the two divergent currents that have characterised subsequent thinking and theorising about countertransference. In 1910, Freud made a profound observation.

"We have noticed", he wrote, "that no psychoanalyst goes farther than his own complexes and resistances permit, and we consequently require that he shall begin his activity with a self-analysis and continually carry it deeper while he is making his own observations on his patients ..." (pp. 141–2).

This statement speaks to a fundamental issue for all analysts: the limitations that our own neuroses, our own blind spots, and our own character issues impose on our ability to understand, and respond to, communications from another person. Viewing counter-transference as unconscious forces arising in the analyst that impede his ability to receive and correctly understand those communications, Freud recognised that unless the analyst can work with himself to overcome those blocks and scotomas that, years later, McLaughlin (1988) characterised as our "hard spots and dumb spots", the analysis will be severely compromised and, in fact, effectively stalemated by these unrecognised aspects of the analyst's psychology.

While Freud's early emphasis on the importance of self-analysis occurred prior to the establishment of the training analysis as the prime means for helping analysts overcome their neurotic conflicts and the countertransference reactions that spring from them, the idea that, ultimately, every analyst is left to contend with the powerful, and potentially disruptive, unconscious forces unleashed in him or her by the process of analysing remains an insight of fundamental importance. Today with the freer and more sponta-neous use of the analyst's subjectivity emphasised by a number of analysts (Renik, 1993), Freud's recognition of the enduring nature of countertransference and of the fact that it exists as an ever-present force in analytic work has taken on fresh significance. Under-emphasised by certain contemporary authors, the notion that countertransference not infrequently acts as an impediment to understanding and a block to progress was one that was central to Freud's thinking.

Another observation of Freud's, however, was at the root of the opposite view of countertransference; the idea that countertransfer-ence is not only inevitable in analysis, but that as a pathway to understanding the unconscious of the patient it plays an indis-pensable role in treatment. This view of countertransference, which informs much current thinking, has a long history in analysis, which, in this communication, I will touch on only briefly. Its origins can be traced to Freud's recognition that analysis involves communication between the unconscious of patient and analyst and that the transmission, beneath their surface exchanges, of uncon-scious messages between the two participants constitutes an essential part of the analytic process. This fundamental insight, conveyed in Freud's (1912) advice to the analyst to attune his unconscious to that of the patient as a telephone receiver is attuned to the transmitting apparatus, not only paved the way for the seminal idea, articulated by Heimann (1950), that countertransference contains the unconscious of the patient, but through the choice of metaphor implicitly conveyed the notion that unconscious transmission in analysis is a two-way street.

Freud's efforts, early in the century, were devoted to developing theories of unconscious mental functioning that could explain the clinical pictures that confronted him daily and, as a consequence, he focused primarily on the psychology of the patient. His appreciation, however, of the fact that the unconscious of patient and analyst are in continual contact and that covert messages are continually transmitted between the two participants opened the way to the idea, now increasingly accepted, that analysis inevitably involves the interplay of two psychologies.

A number of writers (Tyson, 1986; Slakter, 1987) have pointed out that Freud viewed countertransference solely as an obstacle in analysis and a problem of the analyst's that had to be overcome. He spoke quite directly, they point out, of the importance of the analyst's mastering his countertransference.

There is little doubt that this attitude developed, in large part, in response to the threat to the public image of analysis that stemmed from the behaviour of certain of Freud's colleagues. Ferenczi, Jung and other key figures were engaged in troubling involvements with patients and/or the families of patients, and Freud himself is reported to have confided to Ferenczi that he nearly succumbed to the charms of a female patient. Moreover, Freud remembered well how, in response to Anna O's erotic transference feelings, his old friend, Joseph Breuer, fled the field in panic.

Clearly danger existed, and as the leader of a nascent movement Freud understood that it was necessary for him to take a stand against the inappropriate behaviour that threatened its very existence. Whether he also recognised anything positive in countertransference is uncertain, but there is some evidence that he grasped its potential usefulness. Tyson (1986) points out that in a letter to Jung in response to the latter's involvement with Sabina Spielrein, Freud (1909) remarked that although they must be dominated, the analyst's sexual and loving feelings for patients can help him develop a thick skin and learn how to displace his affects in a clinically useful way. Thus, he said, such countertransference feelings constitute a "blessing in disguise" (p. 231).

It was Ferenczi (1919), however, who spoke most directly of the inevitability of countertransference and of the idea that it is valuable in understanding the patient. In fact, partly in rebellion against his old mentor, Ferenczi took issue with Freud's notion that countertransference must always be mastered. Efforts to do so, Ferenczi pointed out, may cause the analyst to constrain or inhibit his free-floating mental processes. And such free-ranging processes in the analyst, he believed, are essential elements in analytic listening and in the attainment of empathic understanding.

Appreciating, as few did before him, the central role that countertransference plays in treatment, the critical impact that it can have on the analytic process, and the fact that patients often have an intuitive awareness of the analyst's emotional responses, Ferenczi (1919) advocated disclosure of certain of the analyst's subjective experiences. He also experimented with mutual analysis, with the patient, for a time, becoming the analyst's analyst.

In addition to whatever personal motivations led him to undertake this experiment, Ferenczi believed that the analyst could learn much about himself from the patient and that the patient could benefit from understanding how the analyst's personality and conflicts have affected his thought processes and the material that emerges in sessions. In different form, some of these ideas are currently being investigated by colleagues (Aron, 1991; Ehrenberg, 1992), who are interested in the way in which the covert transmission of unconscious affects and fantasies influences the analytic process.

Radical for their time and perceived by Freud and his circle as potentially dangerous ideas, Ferenczi's views remained for many years outside the mainstream of classical analysis. Regarded for the most part as the product of a creative, but troubled, individual whose personal needs contaminated his thinking, Ferenczi's work was largely ignored by traditional analysts in the US. Rarely were his papers read in the classical American institutes, and when one was assigned, it was usually recommended as a matter of historical interest, rather than as a significant contribution to theory or technique.

In recent years there has been some revival of interest in Ferenczi in the US. A biography of him recently appeared and, not infrequently, his views are cited in papers and presentations. This new interest in Ferenczi stems, I believe, from several sources. Certain contemporary analysts, interested in the intersubjective and social constructivist views of analysis, find in him a kindred spirit; one who, in their view, was, like themselves, regarded by the reigning powers as an outsider and a non-conformist. It is also true in the US, however, that in response to the shift that has taken place towards greater appreciation of the interactive dimension of analysis and the fluidity and permeability of the transference–countertransference relationship, a number of classically trained analysts have wanted to take a second look at some of Ferenczi's views. Whereas not many years ago his ideas were regarded as little more than rationalised enactments of personally driven beliefs, a number of colleagues today are finding in them an appreciation of the role of meta-communications in analysis and of the interplay between the minds of patient and analyst that was quite remarkable for its time.

Of course not all of Ferenczi's contributions are regarded as having equal value, and, in fact, many analysts of the classical school continue to view his thinking as naïve and misguided. Traditional analysts, who are critical of the so-called contemporary Freudians, not infrequently point out that many of their ideas, far from being original, are simply applications and restatements of Ferenczi's old, well-worn and long-discarded notions.

One of his ideas that not infrequently comes in for severe criticism is a formulation of the analytic process that Ferenczi put forward in 1920. At that time, he conceived of analysis as essentially a corrective emotional experience, one in which the analyst's sincere and caring interest in his patient provides an opportunity for the reworking and correction of emotional trauma experienced in early childhood. As is well known, the idea of a corrective emotional experience in any form has long been a bête noir for traditional analysts. The fact that Ferenczi (1920) endorsed this view has been used by certain traditional analysts to discredit not only this idea, but his work in general. Moreover, responding to certain similarities between Ferenczi's thinking and that of contemporary analysts interested in intersubjectivity and ignoring their equally important differences, these critics regard many of the current developments in analysis simply as repetitions of Ferenczi's mistakes.

Whatever one's view of these matters, however, it is clear that as a pioneer in exploring the interactive nature of countertransference, the way in which transference and countertransference interweave in the analytic process, and the fact that patients often intuitively grasp, and are affected by, covertly transmitted aspects of the analyst's attitudes and feelings, Ferenczi both anticipated and influenced much contemporary thinking.

It was not only Ferenczi, however, who anticipated certain current ideas about countertransference. A number of writers raised issues that, today, are at the forefront of current discussion and debate. Stern (1924) spoke of two kinds of countertransference; that stemming from the analyst's personal conflicts, and that arising in response to the patient's transference. It is the latter, Stern said, that is useful in analysis. The former constitutes an obstacle to understanding. To use himself effectively, Stern maintained, the analyst must meet the patient's transference with a transference of his own; that is, his approach must not be too intellectual, not too focused on cognitive understanding. Rather, he must permit his feelings and fantasies to arise and must allow his unconscious to resonate with that of the patient in order to grasp the latter's unconscious communications. This perspective embraces much that was to come later, including Isakower's (1963a) notion of the analytic instrument, Reich's (1951) concern with the neurotic aspects of countertransference, and Sandler's (1976) idea that, optimally, the analyst functions not only with freely hovering attention (Freud, 1912), but with free-floating responsiveness.

Deutsch (1926) also spoke of the way in which the analyst receives and utilises the patient's material. The patient's associations, she held, become an inner experience for the analyst. This mode of processing the material, which gives rise to fantasies and memories on the part of the analyst, is, she claimed, the basis for all intuition and intuitive empathy. It is not enough, however, Deutsch said, for the analyst to sift the patient's material through his unconscious. He must also process the data intellectually in order to arrive at proper understanding. This view foreshadows the position of Arlow (1993) who believes that conscious processing of the data must be added to the analyst's intuition and unconscious mental operations in order for accurate interpretations to be formulated. It also anticipated the current controversy between those who favour the Deutsch–Arlow view and those, like Renik (1993) who maintain that, being a continuous unconscious influence in analysis, the analyst's subjectivity is inevitably enacted before it reaches consciousness and can be subjected to the kind of cognitive processes that Arlow (1993) describes.

Other authors, too, anticipated current issues in countertransference. By pointing out that the patient's psychosexual conflicts evoke developmentally similar conflicts in the analyst, Glover (1927) was touching on an issue that is much discussed today; the way in which the patient's material resonates with and evokes memories of parallel psychological experiences in the analyst (McLaughlin, 1981; Blum, 1980; Poland, 1986; Jacobs, 1991; Levine, 1997). This issue is currently the subject of neurophysiological research, as well as efforts by analysts to learn how such subjective reactions can best be utilised in the clinical situation. Glover (1927) also attempted to distinguish countertransference proper from counter-resistance in the analyst. While few analysts today believe that such distinctions can be meaningfully made, Glover's interest in the analyst's, as well as the patient's, resistance also foreshadowed a matter of current concern; the way in which resistances are mutually constructed by patient and analyst (Boesky, 1990; Hoffman, 1991).

Strachey (1934) recognised the fact of mutuality in analysis; that is, the interaction of patient and analyst, and he pointed out that the mutative transference interpretation can be effective only when there is an emotional force field (or strong emotional engagement) between patient and analyst. Thus, although he did not refer to countertransference proper, Strachey (1934) helped set the stage for the recognition both of the intersubjective aspects of analysis and the fact that the analyst's emotional participation, expressed, in large measure, through his countertransference responses, is an indispensable element in the therapeutic action of analysis.

Low (1935) anticipated the views of Renik (1993) by taking issue with Freud's contention that countertransference can and should be mastered. This, she believed, was a fantasy, and she argued, not for the exclusion of the analyst's countertransference reactions, but for their use in analysis. It is through the analyst's subjective experiences, she held, that he or she can arrive at a correct understanding of the patient. This latter aspect of Low's position was elaborated and developed in different forms by the British object-relations school, by the Kleinians, and by a number of contemporary American analysts. Thus the idea that the analyst's subjectivity constitutes a valuable pathway to understanding the unconscious of the patient—the central notion that links contemporary views of countertransference—has a long history in psychoanalysis.

Other issues that are at the forefront of modern thinking also arose in the thirties and forties. Balint & Balint (1939) spoke of the question of self-revelation and noted that analysts inevitably reveal much about themselves through their character traits and their ways of working. And they pointed out that patients regularly pick up these cues and, preconsciously, possess a good deal more knowledge about their analysts than may be apparent.

Fliess (1942) used the concept of trial identification, currently an important idea in our understanding of the inner processes of the analyst (Arlow, 1993), and De Forest (1942) not only underlined the importance of countertransference in shaping the analytic experience, but, like Ferenczi (1920), advocated its selective disclosure.

Thus, before the Second World War most of the questions concerning countertransference that have preoccupied analysts today were raised for consideration. Despite this fact and its obvious importance as a central element in the analytic process, for some years countertransference held a peripheral place in the house of psychoanalysis: a concept acknowledged to be important but one not further developed or explored. Perhaps this was partly because that Freud wrote comparatively little about countertransference and, after offering his initial insights, essentially dropped the subject. It also seems, however, to be due to the fact that analysis was concerned with other matters. The assimilation and integration of the structural theory, the development and clinical application of ego-psychology, and the efforts to establish psychoanalysis as a general psychology, among other issues, preoccupied theoreticians and clinicians alike.

Several factors changed this picture. Experience in the Second World War put analysts in touch with a wide variety of mental conditions, particularly trauma and its effects on the personality. This led to a greater interest in working with patients outside the realm of the strictly neurotic. And as analysts expanded their practices to include more of the "widening scope" type of patients, they often found themselves experiencing powerful and troubling emotions evoked by the blatant sexuality, the raw aggression, and other primitive affects directed at them by these patients. It soon became evident that contending with countertransference was a major consideration in working with the borderline and psychotic patients that analysts were now attempting to treat.

It was partly as a result of such experience that Winnicott (1949) published his well-known paper, "Hate in the countertransference". Echoing Ferenczi's contention that some countertransference reactions were objective responses to qualities in the patient and not neurotic in origin, Winnicott not only legitimised countertransference feelings and emphasised the important role that negative countertransferences play in treating disturbed patients, but demonstrated that the evocation of such feelings is a necessary and essential part of the treatment.

This liberating step in the use of countertransference was soon followed by another landmark contribution; a year later, Heimann (1950) argued that countertransference was not only inevitable, it was invaluable because it constituted an essential research tool for the analyst. Articulating a position that since then has been the subject of much controversy, Heimann (1950) viewed the counter-transference as largely the creation of the patient. The analyst's subjective experiences, she believed, were put into him by projections from the patient. Thus what the analyst experiences subjectively can be understood as representing aspects of the patient's mind. This view has had a strong influence on certain conceptions of countertransference, and, in modified form, under-lies the assumption of certain colleagues who view the mechanism of projection and, especially, projective identification as constituting the heart of the countertransference experience.

Another influential contribution appeared about the same time. In 1951, Little published a paper in which she explored the complex nature of the transference–countertransference relationship and pointed out that, inevitably, it contains a mixture of normal and pathological elements derived from the psychologies of both patient and analyst. Exploring the countertransference in more depth than had been done previously, she showed how conflicting motives in the analyst, including his need for reparations for his or her unconscious aggression, will cause him both to wish to cure the patient and to keep him ill. Several years later, Little (1957) followed up this contribution with another in which she focused on the critical role that the analyst's paranoid anxieties and depressive feelings play in treatment, and she maintained that the success of an analysis depended on the satisfactory working through of the analyst's pathology.

Winnicott's (1949) paper and those of Heimann (1950) and Little (1951) had a substantial influence on the future development of the concept of countertransference, particularly in England, South America and in some European countries. Winnicott's approach, which viewed countertransference as induced by projections of the patient's internal objects, was expanded and elaborated by colleagues of the object-relations school (Fairbairn, 1952, 1963; Guntrip, 1961), who, with much sophistication and expertise, explored and mapped this terrain. For them, countertransference became equated with the analyst's total responses, responses which, in large measure, reflected the projected and displaced inner object world of the patient. This view of countertransference is maintained today by many colleagues trained in this tradition and has been the basis for the illuminating contributions of Bollas (1987), Casement (1985), Sandler (1962) and many others.

The key papers of Heimann and Little reflected the views of Melanie Klein (1921–1945), whose influence grew rapidly in post-war England. Klein's emphasis on the continued existence in troubled individuals of primitive schizoid–paranoid mechanisms and the pervasive use of projective identification in such patients contained the corollary ideas that the analyst would inevitably experience the impact of those primitive mechanisms and that the understanding and management of his countertransference responses was at the very heart of the treatment. Although modified and expanded today by more complex and subtle notions about the way in which patient and analyst experience each other as well as by innovative and valuable advances in technique, Joseph (1985), Steiner (1993), the Kleinian view of countertransference has its roots in the idea that the analyst's subjective experiences are primarily, though not exclusively, the product of projective identifications, and that it is the impact on him of the patient's projected paranoid–

schizoid states of mind that constitutes the most important—and potentially most useful—aspect of countertransference.

Although he did not focus on countertransference as such, Bion (1967) emphasised the importance of the analyst's psychology in clinical work. Conceptualising analysis as an undertaking involving the emotional life of two individuals who are engaged in an intense relationship, Bion pointed out that the analyst's attitudes and values are communicated to, and continually influence, the patient and the emerging material. Chief obstacles to effective analytic work, Bion maintained, are the analyst's fantasies of omnipotence, and his tending to cling to theory and to *a priori* knowledge. In this regard, Bion (1967) spoke of the need for the analyst to approach each hour without memory or desire, by which he meant unburdened by subjectivity that prejudices his or her ability to hear and to respond to what the patient is seeking to communicate. Bion was also aware of the analyst's need, like that of the patient, to avoid the pain that not infrequently comes with self-knowledge. In his efforts to minimise pain, Bion pointed out, the analyst may focus on material less troubling to himself as well as to the patient and, in that way, enter in a collusion with him. In indirect ways, Bion's views have influenced the thinking of a number of colleagues, particularly in the Kleinian and intersubjective schools, with regard to the persistent effect of the analyst's countertransferences on the analytic process.

In France, Lacan's (1966) teaching has been an influential force in shaping conceptualisations of the analytic enterprise. With regard to countertransference issues, Lacan pointed out that certain attitudes of the analyst can serve to block the unfolding analytic process. Central among these are the analyst's acceptance of the patient's identification with him, his wish for certainty, and his seeking specific responses from the patient; responses that serve as confirmation of the correctness of his interpretations. Lacan also held that if the analyst seeks to be scientific in the sense of searching for evidence either to formulate or confirm interpretations, such an attitude constitutes an interference to analysis. Effective analytic work, he said, requires open-ended exploration of the way in which the unconscious reveals itself in image, symbol and metaphor. Like Racker (1968), Lacan also pointed out the candidate's wish to please supervisors and teachers and to conform to the prevailing ethos of his analytic institute; attitudes that clearly involve countertransference responses; and that not infrequently derail the analytic work.

In the US, it has been Kernberg (1965, 1976), perhaps more than any contributor, who, in his writings on countertransference, has sought to integrate competing points of view. Drawing on Kleinian and object-relations perspectives as well as the work of Jacobson (1964) on the relationship of self and object, Kernberg has developed a complex and creative view of countertransference that illustrates how the idea of projective identification can be interpreted within an ego-psychological perspective. In addition, he emphasised the idea that unresolved conflicts in the analyst, aroused by the patient's material, constitute an important element in any counter-transference response.

Grotstein's (1981) views are more centrally in the Kleinian–Bionian tradition. His writing focuses less on the contribution of the analyst's neurotic conflicts to countertransference and emphasises, rather, the way in which the patient's aggression, envy, competitive strivings and wish to destroy meaning produces powerful affects in the analyst.

Apart from these two major authors, recent work by Thomas Ogden (1994), which I will comment on shortly, and perhaps a small number of other contributors, American views of countertransference are characterised by a different emphasis and, consequently, a different way of conceptualising the issue. Central to this difference are two factors of overriding importance. The first has to do with the history of psychoanalysis in America after the war. The second related issue concerns the influence of ego-psychology, particularly the ideas of conflict and compromise formation, on the thinking of American analysts.

Following the war, and for some three decades thereafter, analysis in America was dominated by the *émigré* analysts from Europe who had close ties to Freud and the circle of early analysts. To them, analysis, as they had learned it from their teachers, was a precious gift to be preserved, protected against dilution, and handed down to the next generation of students. Their anxiety about the possible contamination of analysis, increased by being in an unfamiliar culture (and one that Freud disliked and found alien to his values) caused them to close ranks and to remain essentially unreceptive to ideas other than those of Freud and those colleagues who were clearly in the Freudian camp.

To these analysts, the ideas of Melanie Klein (1946, 1952) seemed to be the product of fantasy and in the Freud–Klein controversy of the fifties, they lined up solidly on the side of Anna Freud. To them, as to many of the English Freudians, Klein's ideas about the infant's mental states seemed so speculative, so unsubstantiated, and so little capable of proof, that for many years they were not given serious consideration. With few exceptions, Klein was not taught in the curriculum of American institutes and it is only in recent years that there has been greater receptivity to Kleinian ideas and a desire on the part of students to study and understand them.

As for the object-relations perspective, this was regarded as a rather superficial approach, one that sacrificed in-depth understanding of the drives and that underplayed the importance of infantile sexuality. As a consequence, few American students were exposed in any systematic way to the thinking of Winnicott, Fairbairn, Guntrip, or other major contributors of the object-relations school. As a result, for some years many American analysts had only a passing knowledge of the views of these English colleagues and the ways in which they conceptualised the meaning and uses of countertransference.

When, in the early fifties, Heimann and Little published their papers on countertransference, their ideas, clearly influenced by Klein, set off an alarm signal among many Freudians. Instead of countertransference being seen, as Freud viewed it, as an impediment to correct understanding, the concept, as they saw it, was now being elevated to an exalted place by these British analysts and held up as the key to understanding the patient's inner world. Dedicated to the idea that the patient's conflicts could only be approached through careful analysis of ego defences and that countertransference represented the stirring of potentially troubling unconscious conflicts in the analyst, the Freudians in this country strongly opposed these new ideas.

Speaking from the standpoint of classical analysis, Annie Reich responded to the challenge posed by her English colleagues. In a series of papers (1951, 1960, 1966), she clarified the view of countertransference that prevailed among traditional analysts. Acknowledging that countertransference is not only inevitable in analysis but is a necessary ingredient if the analysis is to be emotionally engaged in the work, she reiterated Freud's view that it must be mastered. Countertransference, she said, is not a royal road to the unconscious. Rather, it represents the arousal of conflicts in the analyst that have the effect of interfering with his or her ability to hear and to respond to the patient's communications.

Describing a variety of countertransference responses, Reich (1951) illustrated the way in which long-standing character traits, as well as more immediate countertransference reactions, are not infrequently played out in treatment.

The influence of Reich's papers in America was enormous. For close to two decades the view of countertransference that she held was accepted by traditional analysts in this country. And when the issue was discussed at all in their institutes—by no means a regular occurrence—it was Reich's position that most often was endorsed.

Largely because Reich's (1951) paper solidified the view that countertransference is a problem—more or less severe, depending on the circumstances—that has to be attended to, either through self-examination or further analysis, for some years in this country, a curtain of silence descended on the topic. Since the very word, countertransference, now carried a certain stigma—presumably good analysts had little troubling countertransference and could deal effectively with the little that they had—students were afraid to acknowledge its existence in their case presentations and clinical reports. At the New York Psychoanalytic Institute, typical I believe of the situation that existed in most classical institutes, discussions of countertransference, either in clinical conferences or presentations, were rare. In courses on technique, the issue was touched on but not explored in any depth, (the work of Heimann, [1950], Little [1951] and their predecessors was largely neglected), and if, in supervision, a piece of countertransference behaviour was noted, most often the candidate was advised to take the matter up with his analyst.

The general silence and embarrassment that surrounded the entire question of countertransference at that time extended to the literature. In the late fifties and sixties few articles on counter-transference appeared and, scientifically, the topic seemed to be a dead issue.

There were exceptions to this general trend, however, and in that period, several American analysts made noteworthy contributions to the question of countertransference. Most influential of these was

Otto Isakower (1963a) whose notion of the analytic instrument as belonging to both patient and analyst and as being composed of the temporarily fused unconscious of each, was a highly creative idea that both anticipated later studies concerning unconscious communication and its transmission in analysis (Reiser, 1997; Dahl et al., 1988) and raised questions about technique that are being actively debated today.

Isakower (1963b) stressed the importance of the role of regression in analysis. To communicate effectively, he said, the minds of patient and analyst must be in a state of temporary regression, a condition that is facilitated by the use of the couch, by free association, and by the analyst's stance of expectant silence and evenly hovering attention. Only when these conditions are met, he said, can the instrument operate so that the images, fantasies and memories that arise in the analyst's mind as he listens be meaningfully related to the patient's unconscious.

In contemporary discussions of the issue, Isakower's insight concerning the critical role that regression plays in the positive and creative use of countertransference is often overlooked. Few authors, either in America or abroad, address this important question, which remains an aspect of countertransference that, as yet, has been insufficiently explored.

Several other authors, too, had useful things to say about countertransference. Fromm-Reichmann (1950) echoed Winnicott's (1949) view that countertransference plays an essential role in work with seriously disturbed patients, and she emphasised that the analyst brings his total being, his past as well as his present, to the treatment.

Tower (1956), writing in a vein similar to Little (1951), underscored the interactive nature of the transference–countertransference amalgam and suggested that, in parallel with the transference neurosis, a countertransference neurosis also develops. Thus she conceived of analysis as a dual process, with the unconscious of patient and analyst in continual interaction and the resolution of the transference depending on the analyst's ability to recognise, and to work through, his countertransference neurosis.

Benedek (1953) carried forward the observation made by Ferenczi (1919) and the Balints (1939) that patients have an intuitive awareness of the analyst's attitudes and feelings and she maintained that the latter's personality plays a key role in all that happens in treatment.

Gitelson (1952, 1962), reflecting the influence of Reich's paper and the position of traditionalists in the sixties, became increasingly conservative in his view of countertransference. In an early paper, Gitelson (1952) saw a valuable role for countertransference in the analytic process. He even favoured its selective disclosure to patients as a technique that could advance the analytic process. Ten years later, however, Gitelson took a different stand. Counter-transference, he said then, has a very limited place in treatment. Change, he maintained, occurs primarily through the interpretation of defence, not through the influence of the analyst's personality or, as some colleagues held, through the interaction of the unconscious of patient and analyst.

Like Fromm-Reichman, Searles (1975) was influenced by the interpersonal school and his work focused on the patient's experiences vis-à-vis the analyst. And like Benedek (1953), he noted that patients intuit much about their analysts. In not a few cases, however, he added, the patient, like a child wishing to help a distressed parent, seeks to heal the analyst. And unless he becomes aware of this process and can effectively interpret it, the analyst may collude with the patient, leading to a situation in which the patient becomes entrapped in a neurotic interaction that compromises his autonomy and ability to achieve separation from the parent–analyst.

While valuable in themselves, these various contributions did not stimulate strong interest in the issue of countertransference in America. Nor did they affect the view that, far from being useful, countertransference was a problem to be dealt with personally—and privately—by each analyst; a view that held sway in the US for more than two decades.

The situation was quite different elsewhere. Under the impact of Klein's (1921–1945) ideas and object-relations theory, both of which put a good deal of emphasis on the analyst's subjectivity as a way of accessing the unconscious of the patient, colleagues abroad—especially in England—were far more comfortable with, and knowledgeable about, countertransference than their American counterparts. In fact, the use of countertransference as a way of understanding the inner world of the patient became a regular feature of analytic work both in England and in those countries that were strongly influenced by Kleinian thought.

Chief among these were the Latin American countries. In fact, it was an Argentinian analyst, Heinrich Racker (1958, 1968) who, in pioneering work, opened up many previously unexplored dimensions of countertransference. Making useful distinctions between various types of countertransference responses, Racker showed how certain of these reactions resulted from the analyst's identification with the patient's internal objects, while others developed as consequence of his identification with the patient's drives or ego states. The latter phenomena he termed concordant identifications, while the former were named complementary ones. Racker also distinguished between direct and indirect countertransference reactions. Direct reactions are those which are stimulated by the patient. Indirect countertransference responses arise as more complex phenomena. They represent the analyst's emotional reactions to supervisors, teachers, colleagues or other significant individuals who exert an influence on his way of perceiving and working with his patient. Racker also recognised that the analyst may be influenced in important ways by his reactions to individuals in the patient's world about whom he hears and who evoke memories and fantasies in him. A male analyst, for instance, may develop feelings of rivalry vis-à-vis the spouse of a female patient and in subtle, or not so subtle, ways in which this reactivation of his oedipal conflicts may unconsciously influence his perception of the patient. A similar situation may arise when pre-oedipal conflicts are stimulated in the analyst by the patient's interaction with mothering figures in his life. Racker's recognition of these indirect, but important, dimensions of countertransference opened the way to further exploration and investigation of the phenomena and to the appreciation of the fact that countertransference is a highly complex reaction that condenses and expresses wishes, fantasies, memories, defences and superego prohibitions in a multi-determined way.

Racker's innovative study was influential in two respects. It stimulated interest in countertransference as a phenomenon whose effect on the analytic process was clearly profound, and it set the stage for the development of the view currently held by Hoffman (1991), Stolorow et al. (1983, 1992) and others in the US; that the analytic process entails not only the uncovering of unconscious fantasies and beliefs, but the creation of new psychic realities.

Another South American, Leon Grinberg (1957), extended the Kleinian view of countertransference. He pointed out that, in response to the patient's projective identifications, the analyst reacts with projective identifications of his own. Unlike other Kleinians who, in large measure, viewed countertransference as representing the projected inner world of the patient, Grinberg (1957) emphasised the mutual nature of the projections that take place in intense transference–countertransference reactions. In doing so, he took a step towards broadening the Kleinian view of countertransference and underlined the fact, now increasingly accepted, that countertransference inevitably contains a mixture of elements emanating from both sides of the couch.

It was in the mid- to late seventies that things began to change in America. All at once, as though a dam had broken, a flood of papers on countertransference and related topics began to appear in American journals. Suddenly it became a topic of interest to American analysts and one that, increasingly, became the focus of discussion and debate.

Although seemingly abrupt, this change had been in the making for some time and was the result of a number of interweaving factors. Perhaps the most important of these was the shift in power, influence and control that had gradually taken place on the American analytic scene.

As the influence of the older European analysts diminished with the passage of time, analysts in America became increasingly exposed to ideas outside the Freudian canon. The work of Racker, the English object-relations school, and the Kleinians became more familiar and stimulated interest in the analyst's subjectivity and the way in which it reflected aspects of the patient's inner world. There was greater contact, too, with colleagues in America who were trained in the interpersonal and cultural schools and whose exposure to Sullivan (1953), Thompson (1964), Fromm-Reichmann (1950) and Horney (1939) gave them an understanding of the interactional and intersubjective aspects of analysis that were little emphasised in classical training.

The work of Kohut (1971), too, although much criticised by classical analysts, illuminated an important and commonly experienced countertransference difficulty; that involved in working with highly narcissistic individuals. Kohut's work also demonstrated that empathy—in his view the key element in the analytic instrument—is dependent on the analyst's ability to employ vicarious introspection. He emphasised, in other words, the importance of the analyst utilising his subjectivity, including his countertransference reactions, as a means of understanding the unconscious communications of the patient. Thus, indirectly, Kohut emphasised the indispensable role that countertransference plays in analytic work and, over the years, as aspects of Kohut's thinking became more widely accepted and integrated into the main body of analytic thought, so, gradually, did his view concerning the essential role played in analysis by the analyst's ability to utilise self-reflection and self-monitoring functions in his work.

Equally important, however, was the fact that in the new analytic climate colleagues felt freer to explore their counter-transference reactions, to write about them, and to share them with colleagues. In their institutes, at meetings, and amongst themselves, analysts began to talk more openly about their emotional reactions to patients and to explore the effect that such responses had on the analytic work.

The fact, too, that in allied fields, especially in literature and philosophy, the older positivist views had given way to a new relativism, with emphasis on deconstruction, reader-response criticism and the like, influenced contemporary thinking about psychoanalysis. No longer was the analyst seen as the sole possessor of the truth about the patient's psychology that he conveys through interpretation. Increasingly, the patient was viewed, rather, as a partner in the analytic journey whose insights and intuitions are to be respected, and analysis as a project in which, working together and utilising their own subjective experiences, patient and analyst uncover core unconscious fantasies and construct what Spence (1982) has spoken of as narrative truth. Analysts, too, began to re-examine long-held ideas and discovered, not surprisingly, that some of their prized theories and established ways of working contain unacknowledged countertransference responses to their teachers and training analysts.

In this new climate, there appeared the work of a number of authors who helped stimulate interest in countertransference and such related issues as enactments, intersubjectivity and self-analysis. Important contributors at this time—to name just a few—were Gill (1982), Poland (1986), Schwaber (1983), McLaughlin (1981), Gardner (1983), Boesky (1990), Chused (1991), Stolorow (1983), Ogden (1986) and Renik (1993).

Gill's influence was central. His focus on the analysis of transference, or as he described it, the patient's experience of the analyst, was a major stimulus to the examination, not only of the transference proper, but of the influence that the analyst's subjective reactions had on the patient's perceptions and the material that was linked to those perceptions.

Schwaber's papers (1983, 1992) helped sensitise analysts to the subtleties of the listening process and to the way in which their theories, values, pre-set assumptions and idiosyncratic reactions to aspects of the patient's personality prejudice the way they listen and respond to their patients.

Poland's work (1986, 1988) focused on the way in which patient and analyst operate as a dyad, each a separate individual, but linked through the resonance between their unconscious mental processes. It is because such a dyadic relationship exists, he said—and solely because of its existence—that the analyst can understand the meaning of the patient's associations. Poland's view has much in common with Isakower's (1963a) idea that in analytic hours the unconscious of patient and analyst form a temporary unit that allows for communication to take place between them.

In a series of seminal papers, McLaughlin (1975, 1981, 1988) illustrated the way in which the lives of patient and analyst often intertwine (Blum, 1980) and how subtle enactments of aspects of both of their histories influences the analytic process.

In an original and thought-provoking book, Gardner (1983) described the workings of his mind in analytic hours and, in some detail, illustrated how the memories, and imaginations that surfaced as he listened, were meaningfully linked to the patient's material.

Boesky (1996) has shown convincingly that countertransference enactments are not only inevitable in analytic work, but that they contribute in important ways to the therapeutic action of analysis. While it is essential for such enactments to be analysed, he said, the effectiveness of treatment often depends on the actualisation of certain countertransference responses. Only through this means, he pointed out, can patients gain meaningful understanding of their impact on the analyst and the way in which the transference–countertransference interaction illuminates aspects of their own history.

Chused's (1991) work has been instrumental in developing and clarifying the role of enactments in both child and adult analysis. Like Boesky (1990), she sees enactments as inevitable and potentially useful in illuminating the transference–countertransference relationship. She insists, however, that it is important for the analyst to monitor herself and to make every effort to catch herself in the process of carrying out an enactment. Through such self-reflection, the analyst may be able both to curtail behaviour that is potentially damaging to patients and to gain insight into those communications of the patient that has evoked them.

In his publications, Stolorow (1983, 1992), along with his co-workers, has been at the forefront of efforts to conceptualise the analytic process as an intersubjective one. Taking issue with the traditional view of analysis as essentially a one-person psychology, Stolorow has argued that the subjective worlds of both patient and analyst are mobilised in analysis, that they are in continuous communication, and that both exert an ongoing influence on all that transpires in the analytic process. These ideas, although often criticised by traditional analysts as too much focused on object relations and as not taking the drives and infantile sexuality into account, have been influential in helping to shape certain current views of analysis.

Highly creative, Ogden's (1983, 1997) work has contributed an interesting perspective to thinking about countertransference. Drawing on the Kleinian concept of projective identification, he has focused on the analyst's reveries as a valuable source of information about the patient's inner world. He has also developed the concept of the analytic third (Ogden, 1994), the term he uses to designate those ideas, beliefs and imaginations jointly created and shared by patient and analyst. This shared set of ideas has psychic reality for each and affects the perceptions and thinking of both. Similar to Baranger's (1993) notion of the analytic field, an idea that embraces fantasies and beliefs jointly constructed by patient and analyst, the concept of the analytic third is an original and creative one that focuses on a dimension of the analytic situation that has yet to be fully explored.

Ogden (1994) has also shown convincingly how actions on the part of the analyst, often carried out unconsciously, function as interpretations and are received by the patient as such.

Schafer (1959) has demonstrated how, over time, the analyst builds up a picture of the patient and the patient's inner world that inevitably mixes and fuses with aspects of the analyst's history. The picture that he constructs aids the analyst in creating a narrative that helps the patient organise and understand his psychological experiences.

In recent years, Schafer's (1997) lucid explanations of the work of the new Kleinians, such as Joseph (1985), Steiner (1993), Feldman (1993), and Spillius (1993), has been instrumental in familiarising American analysts with the thinking of these writers. Their emphasis on the importance of the here-and-now interaction of patient and analyst, on the use of the analyst's subjectivity (especially as it relates to the impact of the patient's projective identification on the analyst) and on investigation of the patient's fantasies about the analyst, have had a growing impact on technique among many American colleagues.

A key figure in the current discussions and debates concerning countertransference and the role of the analyst's subjectivity is Owen Renik. Few authors in recent times have aroused as much controversy as has Renik, who, during the past several years, has taken issue with many of the concepts that traditional analysis has long held sacrosanct.

Questioning the validity of such concepts as neutrality, abstinence and objectivity, Renik (1993a, 1995) maintains that the analyst's subjectivity is an inherent and irreducible part of the analytic process. As such, it exerts a continual influence on that process. Given this reality, Renik argues, the concept of counter-transference really has no meaning. The analyst's subjectivity infuses the treatment, making the notion of countertransference redundant.

Enacted unconsciously in all that the analyst thinks and does, including behaviour that he may believe to be neutral and/or objective, the subjectivity of the analyst, Renik says, cannot be identified or controlled prior to its being enacted. Inevitably it will be lived out by the analyst in ways both obvious and subtle. Rather than attempt the unrealisable task of monitoring and controlling his subjectivity, the analyst, Renik believes, is better advised to make it part of the analytic work. The analyst's enactments, in other words, he maintains, must be brought into the analysis, discussed, and their impact on the patient and the analytic work thoroughly understood.

Renik also believes that it is important for the analyst to share certain of his ideas, opinions and perceptions with patients so that they can be openly discussed in treatment. Arguing that analysts simply deceive themselves when they contend that their attitudes, values and beliefs are not communicated to patients, Renik maintains that quite the opposite is true. Whether he likes it or not, the analyst's subjectivity is transmitted to the patient in many ways and on many levels in treatment. Since this is so, Renik says, it is far better for the analyst to bring his views into the open so the patient can evaluate them and assess the impact that they have had on him.

Renik's views have been vigorously disputed by many of his colleagues who believe that in his challenge to classical analysis he has thrown out much that is valuable, that has stood the test of time, and that, in fact, constitutes the core of the method. Renik's iconoclastic ideas, however, have had the undeniably useful effect of stimulating active discussion and debate about the nature of the analytic process and about which ideas and methods in the classical tradition are worth preserving and which should now be discarded.

Although Renik's challenge to the idea of countertransference is a strong and persistent one, he is not the only one who has questioned the usefulness of the term. Some years ago, McLaughlin (1981) took a similar stand. Contending that countertransference has become a term so loosely and imprecisely used today that it has lost much of its value, McLaughlin proposed that we eliminate it altogether and speak of the analyst's transferences. While quite logical and potentially clarifying, this suggestion has not been widely adapted.

It seems, in fact, that countertransference is a term that is here to stay. Like its counterpart, transference, it is an established part of our lexicon, and, although interpretations of it differ—it is under-stood in a broad, totalistic way by some colleagues, more narrowly by others—it is generally agreed that the term refers to those emotional reactions in the analyst that are evoked by aspects of the patient, including his transference. In its emphasis on response to the patient, countertransference differs from the broader term, the analyst's subjectivity, which may include aspects of the analyst's psychology (such as his reactions to pain from a physical injury) which, although they may influence and be influenced by the patient's material, arise independently of them.

Even as generally understood, however, there is much about the concept of countertransference that remains unsettled and problematic. Is it true, for instance, as some colleagues maintain, that countertransference can be understood primarily, if not exclusively, as consisting of projected aspects of the patient's internal world? Is projective identification the main mechanism through which countertransference comes into existence? And is it true that countertransference contains primarily projected aspects of those early mental states designated by Klein (1946) as the schizoid–paranoid position?

It would seem, too, that although modified today, certain notions of countertransference retain Heimann's (1950) idea that a direct channel exists between the unconscious of patient and analyst. In this view, the analyst's inner experiences are products of the patient's mind as projected into the mind of the analyst.

Explicitly, or by implication, some formulations of projective identification endorse this view. Others, however, hold that the patient's projections, no matter how evocative or compelling they may be, are not represented in the analyst's mind in any simple or straightforward way. Increasingly, colleagues of various persuasions are recognising that countertransference, like other aspects of mental functioning, is a complex entity that contains elements derived from the patient's projections, the analyst's psychology, including aspects of his personality and history, and the here-and-now transference–countertransference relationship. In this view, countertransference, like transference itself, is a creation fashioned out of components that shift and change in response to the developing analytic process and changes in the psychology of the analyst.

This view, which draws heavily on the notion of compromise formation and the principle of multiple functioning, is one that underlies much of the thinking about the analytic process in America today. Brenner (1983, 1985), who has been its foremost exponent and explicator, has persuasively discussed the concept of countertransference in these terms.

Another area of controversy concerns the uses of counter-transference and the extent to which the analyst can monitor or control it. Renik's view, as noted previously, is that the analyst's subjective reactions, including his more specific countertransference responses, are inevitably enacted in sessions before they can be consciously apprehended or understood. The idea that, through self-reflection, the analyst can control his countertransference reactions is, he says, a fiction.

In contrast, there is the viewpoint of Jacob Arlow (1993), who represents the position long held by classical analysts. Self-reflection, on the part of the analyst, Arlow maintains, is one of his essential functions. Valuable as they are, he points out, the analyst's intuition and other subjective experiences can provide no more than a clue to what is transpiring in the mind of the patient. The analyst's inner reactions must be monitored and subjected to a cognitive process in which his subjectivity is matched against the evidence provided by the patient's associations. Arlow stresses the importance of utilising image and metaphor, associative links between thoughts, and the contiguity of associations, to obtain the objective evidence needed to confirm and amplify the analyst's intuitions.

Another issue being widely discussed and debated in the US concerns the question of psychological truth and whether, in analysis, it is discovered or created. Authors such as Poland (1988), Chused (1991) and Boesky (1990) hold that while the analyst's countertransference responses often prove useful in helping him gain access to unconscious conflicts in the patient, such reactions do not alter these conflicts. They are, rather, part of the internal world that the patient brings to treatment, and it is the recognition and resolution of such long-standing conflicts that is the central task of analytic work.

Quite different is the position of Irwin Hoffman (1991), whose view of analysis he has labelled a social-constructivist one. Hoffman, like Renik, believes that the analyst's subjectivity is an ever-present force that influences all that happens in analysis. Going beyond Renik, however, Hoffman contends that the analyst's subjective responses not only affect the emerging material, but help create a new psychic reality for the patient. Forged out of the transference–countertransference amalgam, this new reality substitutes and replaces the neurotic compromise formations that are part of the patient's inner world and have been at the root of his troubles. As one can imagine, Hoffman's views, and the idea of analysis that they represent, have been a source of much controversy in America. They extend and expand on the ideas articulated by Spence (1982) and Schafer (1976), who view analytic work as developing narrative, rather than historical truth.

Increasingly discussed and debated, too, is the question of self-disclosure on the part of the analyst and its role in the analytic situation. Until quite recently a taboo, self-disclosure in its many forms has now become a subject of exploration and experimentation.

Arguing that patients perceive much more about their analysts than is apparent in their verbalisations, Aron (1991) believes that active questioning on the part of the analyst about such perceptions opens up previously untapped areas in analytic work and, like Renik, he believes that there is a place, at times, in treatment for a frank and open statement of the analyst's opinions and beliefs. Revealing themselves in this way, these colleagues maintain, does not contaminate the transference, but simply makes explicit what was transmitted in covert and indirect ways.

Other colleagues, too, have begun to explore the possible uses of selective self-disclosure. One of the most articulate of these is Christopher Bollas (1987), who has argued persuasively that judicious sharing with patients of aspects of the analyst's counter-transference responses may open a pathway to certain split-off aspects of their self and object representations that would not be otherwise be accessible.

Ehrenberg (1995), Davies (1994) and Miletic (1998), among others, also support the use of self-disclosure in specific and limited circumstances to enhance the patient's understanding of his projections and long-standing beliefs; and through neurophysiological and clinical studies, Reiser (1997) has demonstrated that memory banks in the analyst are activated by the patient's material. When he is well-attuned to the patient, Reiser maintains, the analyst's memories are meaningfully related to the patient's associations. For Reiser, these findings support Isakower's idea that sharing certain of his inner responses with patients can advance the analytic process.

An interesting area in which the analyst's use of his counter-transference is held to be central to understanding and progress in treatment concerns the analysis of patients who have suffered severe psychological trauma in the early years of life. As McDougall (1979) in France and Mitrani (1995) in the US have shown, such patients are unable to verbalise feelings, and their associations therefore do not provide access to these traumatic experiences. It is only through the analyst's subjective responses as they arise in sessions that he is able to gain access to the troubled inner world of the patient. Such studies, along with Reiser's investigations and the clinical research of such colleagues as Dahl *et al.* (1988) and Waldron (1997), who are studying the exchanges of patient and analysts in tape-recorded analyses, have verified the essential role played by countertransference in elucidating certain long-buried, and not easily decipherable, aspects of the patient's psychology.

It is clear, then, that the study of countertransference and its uses in treatment is an area that is being actively pursued on a number of fronts today. Over the last twenty years investigations of counter-transference and the larger issue of the mind of the analyst at work have expanded our understanding of the analytic process, the impor-tance of the analyst's subjectivity in that process, and the relationship of the intersubjective aspects of analysis to the intrapsychic world of the patient. In short, in the last two decades of this century analysts have begun a fruitful exploration of an observation made years ago by Freud: that communication between the unconscious of patient and analyst is a central feature of the analytic situation.

As I have noted in this review, this exploration has raised many unanswered questions, has sparked a number of controversies, and in the US has contributed to the tensions and divisions between classical analysts, intersubjectivists, and those who seek to integrate these two perspectives.

There is no question, however, that the explorations of counter-transference and related issues that have been carried out by a number of colleagues over the past two decades have had a significant impact on contemporary views of the analytic process. In large measure because of this work, the idea of psychoanalysis as a two-person psychology (as well as a one-person psychology) has gained wide acceptance and countertransference is no longer viewed primarily as an obstacle to treatment. It is seen, rather, as a complex entity containing the analyst's subjective responses fused and mixed with projected aspects of the patient's inner world.

Arising from the interplay of patient and analyst, countertransference, like other aspects of mental functioning, can best be viewed as a compromise formation. A creation forged out of the interplay of patient and analyst, it is an integral and inherent part of the analytic situation; and, as the work described above amply demonstrates, countertransference not only exerts a continuous influence on the analytic process, but constitutes an invaluable pathway for the investigation of that process.

References

Arlow, J. A. (1993). Two discussions of the mind of the analyst and a response from Madeleine Baranger. *Int. J. Psychoanal.*, 74: 1147–1154.

Aron, L. (1991). The patient's experience of the analyst's subjectivity. *Psychoanal. Dialogues*, 1: 29–51.

Baranger, M. (1993). The mind of the analyst; from listening to interpretation. *Int. J. Psychoanal.*, 74: 15–24.

Balint, M. & Balint, A. (1939). On transference and countertransference. *Int. J. Psychoanal.*, 20: 223–230.

Benedek, T. (1953). Dynamics of the countertransference. *Bulln. Menninger Clin.*, 17: 201–208.

Bion, W. (1967). Notes on memory and desire. *Psychoanal. Forum*, 2: 271–180.

Blum, H. P. (1980). The value of reconstruction in adult psychoanalysis. *Int. J. Psychoanal.*, 61: 39–52.

Boesky, D. (1990). The psychoanalytic process and its components. *Psychoanal. Q.*, 59: 580–584.

Bollas, C. (1987). *The Shadow of the Object. Psychoanalysis of the Unthought Known.* New York: Columbia Univ. Press.

Brenner, C. (1983). Transference and countertransference. In: *The Mind in Conflict.* New York: Int. Univ. Press.

Brenner, C. (1985). Countertransference as compromise formation. *Psychoanal. Q.*, 54: 155–163.

Casement, P. (1985). *On Learning from the Patient.* London and New York: Guilford Press.

Chused, J. (1991). The evocative power of enactments. *J. Amer. Psychoanal. Assn.*, 31: 617–639.

Dahl, H. *et al.* (1988). *Psychoanalytic Process Research Strategies.* Berlin: Springer-Verlag.

Davies, J. M. (1994). Love in the afternoon: a relational reconsideration of desire and dread in the countertransference. *Psychoanal. Dialogues*, 4: 153–170.

De Forest, I. (1942). The therapeutic technique of Sándor Ferenczi. *Int. J. Psychoanal.*, 23: 120–139.

Deutsch, H. (1926). Occult processes occurring during psychoanalysis. In: G. Devereux (Ed.), *Psychoanalysis and the Occult* (pp. 133–146). New York: Int. Univ. Press.

Ehrenberg, D. B. (1992). *The Intimate Edge: Extending the Reach of Psychoanalytic Interaction*. New York: Norton.

Ehrenberg, D. B. (1995). Self disclosure. Therapeutic tool or indulgence? *Contemp. Psychoanal.*, 34: 213–218.

Fairbairn, W. R. D. (1952). *Studies of the Personality*. London: Routledge.

Fairbairn, W. R. D. (1963). Synopsis of an object relations theory of the personality. *Int. J. Psychoanal.*, 44: 224–226.

Feldman, M. (1993). The dynamics of reassurance. *Int. J. Psychoanal.*, 74: 275–285.

Ferenczi, S. L. (1919). On the technique of psychoanalysis. In: *Further Contributions to the Theory and Technique of Psychoanalysis* (pp. 177–189). New York: Basic Books, 1952.

Ferenczi, S. L. (1920). The further development of an active therapy in psychoanalysis. In: *Further Contributions to the Theory and Technique of Psychoanalysis* (pp. 198–217). New York: Basic Books, 1952.

Fliess, W. (1942). The metapsychology of the analyst. *Psychoanal. Inq.*, 11: 211–227.

Freud, S. (1909). W. McGuire (Ed.), *The Freud/Jung Letters*. Princeton, NJ: Princeton Univ. Press, 1974.

Freud, S. (1910). The future prospects of psychoanalytic therapy. *S.E.*, 11.

Freud, S. (1912). Recommendations to physicians practising psycho-analysis. *S.E.*, 12.

Fromm-Reichmann, F. (1950). *Principles of Intensive Psychotherapy*. Chicago, IL: Univ. of Chicago Press.

Gardner, R. (1983). *Self Inquiry*. Boston/Toronto: Little Brown.

Gill, M. (1982). *Analysis of Transference, Volume I*. New York: Int. Univ. Press.

Gitelson, M. (1952). The emotional position of the analyst in the psychoanalytic situation. *Int. J. Psychoanal.*, 33: 1–10.

Gitelson, M. (1962). The curative factors in psychoanalysis: I. The first phase of psychoanalysis. *Int. J. Psychoanal.*, 43: 194–205.

Glover, E. (1927). Lectures on technique in psychoanalysis. *Int. J. Psychoanal., 8*: 311–338.

Grinberg, L. (1957). Projective counteridentification and countertransference. In: L. Epstein & A. Feiner (Eds.), *Countertransference* (pp. 169–191). New York: Jason Aronson, 1977.

Grotstein, J. S. (1981). *Splitting and Projective Identification*. New York: Jason Aronson.

Guntrip, H. (1961). *Personality Structure and Human Interaction*. London: Hogarth Press.

Heimann, P. (1950). On countertransference. *Int. J. Psychoanal., 31*: 81–84.

Hoffman, I. Z. (1991). Discussion: towards a social constructivist view of the psychoanalytic situation. *Psychoanal. Dialogues*, 1: 74–105.

Horney, K. (1939). *New Ways in Psychoanalysis*. New York: Norton.

Isakower, O. (1963a). Minutes of the New York Psychoanalytic Institute faculty meeting, October 14 (unpublished).

Isakower, O. (1963b). Minutes of the New York Psychoanalytic Institute faculty meeting, November 20 (unpublished).

Jacobs, T. (1991). *The Use of the Self: Countertransference and Communication in the Analytic Situation*. Madison, CT: Int. Univ. Press.

Jacobson, E. (1964). *The Self and the Object World*. New York: Int. Univ. Press.

Joseph, B. (1985). Transference: the total situation. *Int. J. Psychoanal., 66*: 447–454.

Kernberg, O. (1965). Notes on countertransference. *J. Amer. Psychoanal. Assn., 13*: 38–56.

Kernberg, O. (1976). *Internal World and External Reality: Object Relations Theory Applied*. New York: Jason Aronson.

Klein, M. (1921–1945). *Contributions to Psychoanalysis*. London: Hogarth Press, 1948.

Klein, M. (1946). Notes on some schizoid mechanisms. *Int. J. Psychoanal., 27*: 99–110.

Klein, M. (1952). Some theoretical conclusions regarding the emotional life of the infant. In: J. Riviere (Ed.), *Developments in Psychoanalysis* (pp. 198–232). London: Hogarth Press, 1952.

Kohut, H. (1971). *The Analysis of the Self*. New York: Int. Univ. Press.

Lacan, J. (1966). *Écrits*. Paris: Seuil.

Levine, H. (1997). The capacity for countertransference. *Psychoanal. Inq., 17*: 44–68.

Little, M. (1951). Countertransference and the patient's response to it. *Int. J. Psychoanal., 32*: 32–40.

Little, M. (1957). "R"—the analyst's total response to his patient's needs. *Int. J. Psychoanal., 38*: 240–254.

Low, B. (1935). The psychological compensations of the analyst. *Int. J. Psychoanal., 16*: 1–8.

McDougall, J. (1979). Primitive communication and the use of counter-transference. In: L. Epstein & A. Feiner (Eds.), *Countertransference* (pp. 267–303), New York: Jason Aronson.

McLaughlin, J. (1975). The sleepy analyst: Some observations on states of consciousness in the analyst at work. *J. Amer. Psychoanal. Assn., 23*: 363–382.

McLaughlin, J. (1981). Transference, psychic reality, and counter-transference. *Psychoanal. Q., 50*: 639–664.

McLaughlin, J. (1988). The analyst's insights. *Psychoanal. Q., 57*: 370–388.

Miletic, M. (1998). Rethinking self-disclosure; an example of the clinical utility of the analyst's self-disclosing activities. *Psychoanal. Inq., 18*: 580–601.

Mitrani, J. (1995). Toward an understanding of unmentalised experience. *Psychoanal. Q., 64*: 68–112.

Ogden, T. (1994a). The analytic third—working with intersubjective clinical facts. *Int. J. Psychoanal., 75*: 3–19.

Mitrani, J. (1994b). The concept of interpretive action. *Psychoanal. Q., 63*: 219–245.

Poland, W. (1986). The analyst's words. *Psychoanal. Q., 55*: 244–271.

Poland, W. (1988). Insight and the analytic dyad. *Psychoanal. Q., 57*: 341–369.

Racker, H. (1958). Counterresistance and interpretation. *J. Amer. Psychoanal. Assn., 6*: 215–221.

Racker, H. (1968). *Transference and Countertransference*. New York: Int. Univ. Press.

Reich, A. (1951). On countertransference. *Int. J. Psychoanal., 32*: 25–31.

Reich, A. (1960). Further remarks on countertransference. *Int. J. Psychoanal., 41*: 389–395.

Reich, A. (1966). Empathy and countertransference. In: *Annie Reich—Psychoanalytic Contributions*. New York: Int. Univ. Press, 1973.

Reiser, M. (1997). The art and science of dream interpretation: Isakower revisited. *J. Amer. Psychoanal. Assn., 45*: 891–906.

Renik, O. (1993). Analytic interaction: conceptualising technique in the light of the analyst's irreducible subjectivity. *Psychoanal. Q., 64*: 585–591.

Renik, O. (1995). The ideal of the anonymous analyst and the problem of self-disclosure. *Psychoanal. Q.*, *64*: 466–495.

Sandler, J. (1976). Countertransference and role-responsiveness. *Int. Rev. Psychoanal.*, 3: 43–47.

Sandler, J. (1987). *From Safety to Superego: Selected Papers of Joseph Sandler*. New York: Guilford.

Sandler, J., & Rosenblatt, B. (1962). The concept of the representational world. *Psychoanal. Study Child*, *17*: 128–145.

Schafer, R. (1959). Generative empathy in the treatment situation. *Psychoanal. Q.*, *28*: 342–373.

Schafer, R. (1976). *A New Language for Psychoanalysis*. New Haven, CT: Yale Univ. Press.

Schafer, R. (1992). *Retelling a Life: Narration and Dialogue in Psychoanalysis*. New York: Basic Books.

Schafer, R. (1997). *The Contemporary Kleinians of London*. Madison, CT. Int. Univ. Press.

Schwaber, E. (1983). Psychoanalytic listening and psychic reality. *Int. Rev. Psychoanal.*, *10*: 379–392.

Schwaber, E. (1992). Countertransference: the analyst's retreat from the patient's vantage point. *Int. J. Psychoanal.*, *73*: 349–361.

Searles, A. (1975). The patient as therapist to his analyst. In: P. Giovacchini (Ed.), *Tactics and Techniques in Psychoanalytic Therapy, Volume II—Countertransference* (pp. 95–151). New York: Jason Aronson.

Slakter, E. (1987). *Countertransference*. New York: Jason Aronson.

Spence, D. (1982). *Narrative Truth and Historical Truth*. New York: Norton.

Spillius, E. (1993). Varieties of envious experience. *Int. J. Psychoanal.*, *74*: 1199–1212.

Steiner, J. (1993). Problems of psychoanalytic technique, patient-centered and analyst-centered interpretations. In: *Psychic Retreats: Pathological Organisations in Psychotic, Neurotic and Borderline Patients* (pp. 131–146). London: Routledge.

Stern, A. (1924). On the countertransference in psychoanalysis. *Psychoanal. Rev.*, 2: 166–174.

Stolorow, R. D. *et al.* (1983). Intersubjectivity in psychoanalytic treatment. *Bulln. Menninger Clin.*, *47*: 117–128.

Stolorow, R. D. *et al.* (1992). *Contexts of Being: The Intersubjective Foundations of Psychological Life*. Hillsdale, NJ: Analytic Press.

Strachey, J. (1934). The nature of the therapeutic action of psychoanalysis. *Int. J. Psychoanal.*, *15*: 127–159.

Sullivan, H. S. (1953). *The Interpersonal Theory of Psychiatry*. New York: Norton.

Thompson, C. (1964). *Interpersonal Psychoanalyses. The Selected Papers of Clara M. Thompson*. New York: Basic Books.

Tower, L. (1956). Countertransference. *J. Amer. Psychoanal. Assn.*, 4: 224–255.

Tyson, R. (1986). Countertransference evolution in theory and practice. *J. Amer. Psychoanal. Assn.*, 34: 251–274.

Waldron, S. (1997). How can we study the efficacy of psychoanalysis? *Psychoanal. Q.*, 66: 283–322.

Winnicott, D. (1949). Hate in the countertransference. *Int. J. Psychoanal.*, 30: 69–75.

2: Countertransference

R. D. HINSHELWOOD, London

... to preoccupy oneself with the dream-material to the exclusion of
a pressing transference re-enactment would merit a certain amount
of self-inspection, on the grounds that the seemingly impersonal
nature of dream-production may afford the analyst the same respite
from unpleasantness as it does the patient. [Glover, 1927, p. 505]

The starting-point of this paper is Kleinian and the "street-map" of
contemporary schools of psychoanalysis revealed in this paper
inevitably reflects this personal view. I start with Klein, and move to
the nearest comparisons, other object-relations views developed in
British psychoanalysis.

The Atlantic divide has been wide in psychoanalysis, and ego-
psychology in its early days shunned British developments. In
recent years there have been several attempts at "escape" from the
strictures of ego-psychology. In my perceptions, those escapes
conform more or less to two groups: self-psychology evolving from
Kohut; and the intersubjectivists (e.g. Ogden, Renik) evolving with
influences from the interpersonalists (Sullivanian) as well as a version
of British object relations. We can also include the contemporary
Freudians of London (Sandler, Fonagy).

Parallel to these developments has been the emerging corpus of Lacanian treatises. My acquaintance with other schools varies, reducing as we go down this list. Consequently, the detail and rigour of the paper also reduces.

History and conceptual overview

The concept of countertransference retains the early meaning that Freud gave it: the neurotic transference of the analyst to the patient. He was not very interested in the issue and according to the index to the *Standard Edition*, Freud makes reference to countertransference in only four passages. He required that it be eliminated by the analyst's self-control. He often pictured his technical approach in the impersonal terms of the steely regard of a surgeon (1909) or even of a telephone receiver (1912). This "rule of abstinence" remains today.

But about fifty years ago, the concept was widened beyond the neurotic aspects of the analyst (Winnicott, 1949; Heimann, 1950; Little, 1951; Reich, 1951; Gitelson, 1952; Milner, 1952; Racker, 1957),[1] and it can now refer to the whole of the analyst's affective responses (Heimann, 1950; King, 1978). It has become an increasingly important technical issue.[2]

How did this change come about?

The disturbance in the analyst began to emerge early on as a specific object of study. For instance, Glover devoted the fourth of his lectures on technique in psychoanalysis in 1927 to counter-transference.[3] He began to think in terms of the way the analyst relates to the patient's emotional state. "We might almost say, 'When in difficulty think of your own repressed sadism'" (p. 510).[4]

He was writing here in a manner characteristic of the style in which British psychoanalysis developed a concern with the relational psychology of the psychoanalytic setting—in other words object-relations psychoanalysis. Fenichel was also open to examining rather than repudiating the analyst's neurotic conflict:

Little is written about the very important practical subject of *countertransference*. The analyst like the patient can strive for direct satisfactions from the analytic relationship as well as make use of the patient for some piece of "acting out" determined by the analyst's past. [1979, p. 183]

This stance recognises the interactive nature of transference and countertransference. The blank-screen view of the analyst's role came under an increasingly penetrating critique from all schools, for example, A. Balint (1936) or Fenichel (1941). The sensitivity to the object relations of the analyst and the specific object relations in the psychoanalytic setting developed strikingly in the 1940s.

The pivotal paper was that of Heimann (1950), which came directly from the awareness of the relational aspects of the analyst's own functioning.[5] Perhaps it was also that after thirty years and more of training analyses,[6] there were still analysts having emotional reactions to their patients. Heimann voiced, perhaps most clearly and persuasively, the recognition that the analyst is not just a "mechanical brain", and put forward the thesis that

> the analyst's emotional response to his patient within the analytic situation represents one of the most important tools for his work. The analyst's counter-transference is an instrument of research into the patient's unconscious. [1950, p. 81]

This one passage turns the countertransference from interference into a principal tool. That alteration is based upon understanding the psychoanalytic setting as a relationship. Racker, influenced heavily by Heimann and Klein, remarked that "transference is the expression of the patient's relations with the fantasied and real countertransference of the analyst" (1957, pp. 307–8). The object-relations approach has added the ordinary affective (or empathic) response to the neurotic ones.

The Kleinian approach

Heimann's use of "the term 'counter-transference' ... to cover all the feelings which the analyst experiences towards his patient" (1950, p. 781) contrasts strikingly with the classical view that countertransference is never anything more than the analyst's resistance and is to be eradicated. Klein remained a truer Freudian in this respect, sceptical of the insights that countertransference could bring. "Klein thought that such extension would open the door to claims by analysts that their own deficiencies were caused by their patients" (Spillius, 1992, p. 61).

Nevertheless Klein's own followers have taken a major part in forging the new view of countertransference, and emphasising the relational aspects of the transference–countertransference (Bion, 1959; Segal, 1975; Rosenfeld, 1987). They contributed a specific line of thought, which is the main focus of this Kleinian account.

Part of the analyst's job is to determine what figure he represents for the patient at any given moment whilst trying to retain his knowledge of who he is for himself. Bion described this vividly when working in a group:

> the experience of counter-transference appears to me to have quite a distinct quality ... The analyst feels he is being manipulated so as to be playing a part, no matter how difficult to recognize, in somebody else's phantasy—or he would do if it were not for what in recollection I can only call a temporary loss of insight, a sense of experiencing strong feelings and at the same time a belief that their existence is quite adequately justified by the objective situation. [1961, p. 149]

His description is apt for the individual setting of psycho-analysis, as well as groups. It prompts several research questions:

How do the analyst's feelings become influenced?

How can we know this if it has the quality of a temporary loss of insight?

How can we use the understanding interpretively?

Unravelling these issues has become everyday analytic work. I shall review this development under the headings, (1) projection, introjection, (2) containment and (3) enactment.

Projection, introjection

Quite soon after Heimann's claims for countertransference, it was widely accepted that the analyst's feelings were a normal part of the analytic setting. Money-Kyrle (1956) took up the view that ordinary processes of interaction between persons are mediated by the intrapsychic processes of projection and introjection (Heimann, 1943).[7] Even everyday conversation consists of putting feelings into the listener and their willingness to have that experience in their mind. We talk colloquially of "putting something across", or "giving so-and-so a piece of my mind", etc. In Rosenfeld's words, "A prerequisite of psychoanalytic treatment is that it is necessary to make enough contact with the patient's feelings and thoughts to feel and experience oneself what is going on in the patient" (1987, p. 12).

Money-Kyrle described the patient's attempts in an analysis to convey to the analyst his distress and disturbance in such a way that the analyst is actually in receipt of the disturbance. It is necessary that the analyst feel the disturbance, and can thus be said to become disturbed himself. This may simply be called empathy, but this line of work investigated the mechanisms upon which empathy is based—projection (by the patient) and introjection (by the analyst). A normal process consists of cycles of these mechanisms. Money-Kyrle described, "what seems to be happening when the analysis is going well": "I believe there is a fairly rapid oscillation between introjection and projection. As the patient speaks, the analyst will, as it were, become introjectively identified with him, and having understood him inside, will reproject him and interpret" (1956, p. 23).

Conveying experience like this is not merely in the words. "I am angry" can be said with force and threat, or in a joking fashion, or with blank lack of conviction. The phrase can carry a number of emotional tones. These emotional components are received directly and intuitively and not in the form of verbal statements.

> I had been delayed for two to three minutes at the beginning of a session, at eight o'clock in the morning. My patient said, immediately she was on the couch, "You don't want to see me today". This could be taken in a number of ways: she was angry, she was wounded by my neglect, she was expressing a customary loneliness ... But I sensed a teasing quality, as if she was chiding a friend. The contact therefore felt good, even a little intimate, despite my neglect. I said she seemed a little jocular about it. She denied this, saying she was bitter.
>
> I was left at that point with a verbal statement of her emotional state—bitterness—but on the other hand, I had my sense of a jocular intimacy that was not in the words, but in non-verbal cues. I had a choice: to dismiss my own feelings about the communication as my

aberration, or to register it as a potential communication, probably unconscious.

Shortly afterwards in this session she told me a dream, which I won't relate, but the associations involved a great deal of description of happy families around the breakfast table, as often shown in television advertising. She was a little disbelieving and contemptuous of this portrayal of family life.

I could recognise that she was using her associations to deal with her phantasies that my family had delayed me at our happy breakfast table, from which she was excluded. She was contemptuous and instead, unconsciously substituted her own jocular intimacy in place of my family.

When I put this to her, she said, sourly, "Of course you would say something like that". This was said with much more wounding intent than her original comment about my lateness. This subsequent interpretation of her oedipal exclusion felt like a rejection of her seduction and left her more in touch with feeling cruelly alone, and allowed her (perhaps more honestly) to express her sour rejection of me.

Thus my feelings, the sense of a teasing quality in her first words, led me to reflect on her own account of her emotional state. It was not exactly an empathic response of mine. Or rather, if it was empathic, it led to something that was initially out of reach. In that sense, my affective response added considerably to the listening I was actually doing at that moment. It added a route into a possible unconscious state of affairs that formed organised defences against oedipal issues.

This is an ordinary example of a communication that came from a direct effect of one person upon another. The analytic situation enables us to understand the process in slow motion as it were, and guided by the analyst's feelings.

Starting with this "normal" involvement of the analyst's feelings Money-Kyrle then moved on to deviations from the normal. The analyst, he says, unfortunately

> is not omniscient. In particular, his understanding fails whenever the patient corresponds too closely with some aspect of himself which he has not yet learnt to understand ... when that interplay

between introjection and projection, which characterizes the analytic process, breaks down, the analyst may tend to get stuck in one or other of these two positions. [1956, pp. 361–2]

In the first of these stuck positions, ill-understood aspects of the patient remain inside the analyst and burden him.

Then, the risk is that these aspects of the patient's experience, together with uncomprehended aspects of the analyst, will be projected into the patient. Then he becomes stuck in the second, the projective position. He will experience a sense of depletion, "often experienced as the loss of intellectual potency" (p. 362) and he may become confused and feel stupid.

Money-Kyrle described a process in a session that started with the patient feeling useless and despising himself for that. The analyst felt somewhat at sea during the session and the patient showed increasing rejection and contempt for his interpretations. By the end of the session the patient no longer felt useless, but angry: "It was I who felt useless and bemused" the analyst reported (1956, p. 363). The analyst was sufficiently disturbed by the patient's abuse of him that it was only after the session when "I eventually recognized my state at the end [was] so similar to that he had described as his at the beginning" (p. 27). The projection by the patient and the introjection by the analyst is clear. But the result on the analyst's mind is that he could not recognise what was happening until he was out of the presence of the projecting patient. His own mind was too disturbed to continue functioning properly for that moment.

Brenman Pick took this further. She described how aspects of the patient's experience are being projected into some *specific* aspect of the analyst. She described this as a "mating of minds". For example,

the patient projects into the analyst's wish to be a mother ... patients touch off in the analyst deep issues and anxieties related to the need to be loved and the fear of catastrophic consequence in the face of defects, i.e. primitive persecutory or superego anxiety. [1985, p. 161]

This is not merely a phenomenon of disturbed patients. In Brenman Pick's view, "If there is a mouth that seeks a breast as an inborn potential, there is, I believe, a psychological equivalent, i.e. a state of mind which seeks another state of mind" (p. 157). She gave the following example:

> Consider a patient bringing particularly good or particularly bad news; say, the birth of a new baby or a death in the family. Whilst such an event may raise complex issues requiring careful analysis, in the first instance the patient may not want an interpretation, but a response; the sharing of pleasure or of grief. And this may be what the analyst intuitively wishes for too. Unless we can properly acknowledge this *in* our interpretation, interpretation itself either becomes a frozen rejection, or is abandoned and we feel compelled to act non-interpretively and be "human". [p. 160]

This warns of the twin problems, the Scylla and Charybdis, of the countertransference—emotional freezing like the steely surgeon;[8] or being over-human and seduced out of role (ultimately, perhaps, to unethical relations).

The analyst is required to pay attention to this intimate linking, or "mating", between the patient and herself. Disentangling this entanglement is what Brenman Pick calls "working through in the countertransference".[9] Money-Kyrle specified that this working through entailed

> three factors to consider: first, the analyst's emotional disturbance, for he may have to deal with this silently in himself before he can disengage himself sufficiently to understand the other two; then the patient's part in bringing this about and finally its effect on [the patient]. Of course, all three factors may be sorted out in a matter of seconds, and then indeed the counter-transference is functioning as a delicate receiving apparatus. [1956, p. 361]

It is of some importance that we make this distinction between normal countertransference, when the analyst can make the distinction between his own disturbance and his patient's, and when the analyst gets into trouble.

Containment

A different way of describing the nature and process of the analyst's disturbance was initiated by Bion whose elaboration has the advantage of offering as a model one familiar to psychoanalysis—

the model of the mother with infant. He elaborated this view as the "container and contained".

> The analytic situation built up in my mind a sense of witnessing an extremely early scene. I felt that the patient had witnessed in infancy a mother who dutifully responded to the infant's emotional displays. The dutiful response had in it the element of impatient "I don't know what's the matter with the child." My deduction was that in order to understand what the child wanted the mother should have treated the infant's cry as more than a demand for her presence. [1959, pp. 312–3]

An infant needs something other than duty from a mother. It needs a mother who can feel the disturbance, and to a degree become disturbed herself.

> From the infant's point of view she should have taken into her, and thus experienced, the fear that the child was dying. It was this fear that the child could not contain ... An understanding mother is able to experience the feeling of dread that this baby was striving to deal with by projective identification, and yet retain a balanced outlook. [Bion, 1959, p. 313]

This emotional, non-verbal interaction, characteristic of infant and mother, has become a model of the core analytic relationship. The knack is to *feel* the dread and still retain a balance of mind. Segal endorsed this function:

> The mother's response is to acknowledge the anxiety and do whatever is necessary to relieve the infant's distress. The infant's perception is that he has projected something intolerable into his object, but the object was capable of containing it and dealing with it. He can then reintroject not only his original anxiety but an anxiety modified by having been contained. He also introjects an object capable of containing and dealing with anxiety. [1975, pp. 134–5]

The function of taking in, dealing with, and letting the infant know about the distress is now generally called "containing". In this view an emphasis is placed on what happens inside the person into which the projection of distress is put. Sometimes called "digesting" (or metabolising), the important function is a transformation of the distress into an experience of distress tolerated.

But things may go wrong; this mother could not "tolerate experiencing such feelings and reacted either by denying them ingress, or alternatively by becoming a prey to the anxiety which resulted from introjection of the infant's feelings" (Bion, 1959, p. 313).

These two alternatives connect with the psychoanalyst's problems described earlier—either freezing, or moving out of role. The consequence is that the infant "re-introjects, not a fear of dying made tolerable, but a nameless dread" (1962, p. 116). Using this model, the analytic setting comprises a similar container—*introjecting the patient's distress, "digesting" it and converting it into a verbal container* that is then communicated as speech in the form of an interpretation.

In the following vignette the patient experiences himself in relation to an object in the analysis and internally (his remembered "mother") which "denies him ingress". The object turns away from his neediness which the patient then believes, guiltily, is an intolerable burden to the object.

This 35-year-old man had commenced analysis with quite a paranoid fear of being attacked. This had quickly taken the form of an anxiety in the analysis that my opinions put into his mind would obliterate his, and him.

He started one session telling me he had not written a cheque for the bill I had given him the session before. He had come straight on to me this morning after a night shift he had started temporarily. He felt different today compared with when he came from home. After five minutes' silence, he said a relative had told him a story about his mother passing a homeless man on the street and she refused to give money. He implied this was very callous.

This view of his mother was familiar: someone who was distracted in her mind by other thoughts and problems she had.

I said it was a complicated situation: he was clearly distracted by his work from my need expressed in my bill, but he then felt guilty about it, as if he was like his mother not giving to the homeless beggar in me. But I became aware that I was keen to interpret this link.

He responded in a slightly lofty way that he thought what a sumptuous area of London I live in. This may have been a simple denial, but I thought it carried something else. I wondered if my keenness to make the interpretive link felt to him as if I wanted to take over, so that he felt in danger of being obliterated. Perhaps I had indeed been a bit quick and realised that perhaps it was because I thought his announcement about the cheque had been a bit unapologetic.

As I was trying to capture this thought in my mind, he had gone on to another thought. He told me he had seen a beggar in the street on the way to me today. He said this factually as if he expected me to recognise a link with the earlier story of someone homeless. A moment later, he said it was more that he was worried about his own neediness.

I then made an interpretation based on an assumption that turned out to be incorrect. I assumed the conflict was about accepting an insight about neediness. So, I talked to him about the neediness in him, in the beggar, in me and in the people whom he looked after on the night shift. I was aware of feeling some satisfaction with this interpretation.

He responded characteristically. Being with me, he said, was always like hitting a brick wall. I believed then that my assumption had been wrong. His conflict at that moment was not so much about insight into his neediness. Instead it was still his fight with an object in me, a mother with a brick-wall mind that ignored his, and was pleased with my own thoughts that I put into him.

I said he felt at that moment I was distracted by the importance of my own ideas, and, from what he had said, I reminded him of a mother who had no room to think about him.

Quite strikingly his moment of resentment vanished. He clearly felt remembered by this interpretation, and he then addressed his feelings of being under attack. It was not simply his neediness, but that when in need he was attacked by a mind that blotted him out.

This patient is acutely sensitive to whether the person he is with has a mind that is open to his distress. The moments I record demonstrate, I claim, an interaction in which I did in fact have certain feelings of my own, to which I reacted. In this sense I could enact with him an irritable intrusion into his mind.

When my patient tried to use my mind as a place to put aspects of his own experience, he found, like Bion's, that my mind refused to accept his experiences and his needs. This patient is occupied with an object that turns away from his needs and makes him feel guilty for burdening the mother in me.

However, at one point, I grasped this problem sufficiently for him to feel that his fears were in fact grasped, and his manner changed as he discovered his own capacity to think about it. My verbal elaboration in this instance did contain the immediate moment of distress, and he did regain his capacities for thinking about it and understanding himself for a while.

When, as here, things "go wrong", the patient is then confronted with an analyst who does not contain distress. Often then the patient is concerned about what happens to the analyst's mind as the patient projects intolerable experiences (Hinshelwood, 1985). Interpretations of this state of affairs may then be of two kinds. Either the analyst might directly show the patient his projections into the analyst or he might describe the patient's phantasies of threat and damage to the analyst.[10] The latter points to the patient's experience of the analyst's contribution. Steiner remarked on this occurrence:

> At these times the patient's most immediate concern is his experience of the analyst ... I think of these interpretations as *analyst-centred* and differentiate them from *patient-centred* interpretations ... In general, patient-centred interpretations are more concerned with conveying understanding, whereas analyst-centred interpretations are more likely to give the patient a sense of being understood. [1993, p. 133]

If the state of the analyst's mind occupies the patient then that is the immediate anxiety in the session and that needs to be addressed by interpretation if possible. It is so, even if the patient's phantasy is not correct about the analyst, because it is true for the patient.

These interpretations of the patient's phantasies about the analyst's feelings can be elaborated with a "because" clause, indicating that the analyst's state of mind has arisen because of the particular effect of the patient. However, this can lead to difficulties, at least at first, before the patient is ready. Then the patient can feel intruded upon rather than understood. For one of Steiner's patients,

when *patient-centred* interpretations implied that she was responsible for what happened between us [then] she became most
persecuted and tended to withdraw. It was particularly over the
question of responsibility that she felt sometimes I adopted a
righteous tone which made her feel that I was refusing to examine
my own contribution to the problem and unwilling to accept
responsibility myself. [1993, p. 144]

Responsibility is a key trigger for depressive anxiety, and some
degree of working through of that position may have to be achieved
before the patient's role in the phantasy can be interpreted. That is
to say, the patient's responsibility for the analyst's mind brings a
feeling of guilt and blame, which may involve a sense of deserving
punishment.[11] It is a key technical question whether this responsibility should be interpreted, or whether the patient should be
spared this sense of responsibility and guilt, as Steiner suggests. Or
rather, we need to judge the degree of responsibility the patient can
bear without this interfering with his ability to go on reflecting
within the analytic process.

Enactment

One aspect of containment is the pressure it puts the analyst under
to actually perform the role of the patient's transference figure.[12]
Joseph starts with the task of

> looking at the way in which patients use us—analysts—to help
> them with anxiety. After all, the reason which brings patients into
> analysis is fundamentally that they cannot manage anxiety. Though
> it does not of course mean that the patient is consciously aware of
> this. [1978, p. 223]

The patient's view of the cure that he needs may not be the same
as ours. In fact, that conflict is usual, especially if the patient
fundamentally believes that the distress is unmanageable by
anyone. Then they will expect, usually unconsciously, that we will
perform according to their expectation of a joint evasion (Feldman,
1997).

Then we often do in fact find ourselves pressed into actually
enacting roles. It is only by reflecting on what we have got ourselves
into that we can then understand the patient's side of this and our

own—and this can inform us of exactly what is to be evaded or what satisfactions and excitements we are expected jointly to indulge in. Commenting on Joseph's work, Feldman & Spillius write:

> The pressure that analysts may feel under to ease the pain, often by some form of activity (such as answering questions, giving reassurance, or giving explanations) whose tacit meaning to the patient is that the analyst cannot stand the pain either. [1989, p. 50]

Then the analyst is provoked towards defensive moves that have the quality of actions—to do something to change the relationship—rather than to articulate the pain of it. Joseph described a vignette indicating the way in which she felt the patient was requiring her to play a part in one of his phantasies:

> Patient A. begins a session by telling me that once again he has been extremely nasty with his wife on the previous night and he enumerates a series of apparently unkind, intolerant things that he has done and his wife's responses. It sounds from this that he might be experiencing what we would call super-ego anxiety ... Or he might be speaking about his anxiety about his wife and her ruthlessness and the bad state of the marriage ... Or, is he telling me about the failure of my work ... Or is it to be understood as an acting out from the relationship with the analyst? [1978, p. 223]

There are various possible meanings, or sub-meanings, inherent in the communication. She goes on to describe how her own experience in the session contributes to deciding between these meanings:

> Actually from my sense of what was going on, from the way in which the patient was talking and the atmosphere that was being created in the session, it seemed to me that the most important aspect was the patient's attempt to involve me in a kind of ... beating of him ... the attempt here is to get the analyst to act out with the patient, to be disturbed, critical, annoyed. [p. 223]

The analyst comes to know about this exciting beating phantasy by understanding her own feelings in a particular way.[13] She conveys like Bion that she is recruited (unconsciously) to a particular role. The particular job of the analyst is to identify what role the patient is unconsciously pushing the analyst into. These are joint enactments in the session. They may be very disturbing; and yet again very congenial to the analyst.

The invitation by Joseph's patient to enact the role of a sadistic persecutor was alien. Its ego-dystonic quality enabled the analyst to become fairly quickly aware of this pressure.

However, much more syntonic invitations occur (Feldman, 1997). An intimate relatedness that an analyst is prone to is to perform the role of a good mother. Analytic care is often compared with mothering care. Brenman Pick described a patient who reported an incident after a car accident when the mother put the phone down because she could not stand hearing about the son's accident. The patient has a

> yearning for someone who will not put down the phone, but instead will take in and understand ... this supposes the transference on to the analyst of a more understanding maternal figure. I believe though, that this "mates" with some part of the analyst that may wish to "mother" the patient in such a situation. If we cannot take in and think about such a reaction in ourselves, we either act out by indulging the patient with actual mothering (this may be done in verbal or other sympathetic gestures) or we may become so frightened of doing this, that we freeze and do not reach the patient's wish to be mothered. [1985, p. 159]

Indeed, being like a mother is often a significant motivation to become a psychoanalyst or psychotherapist in the first place. Patients may correctly spot this. So, extending such an example, the bad aspects of mothering are relegated to family, spouse and past objects etc., away from the session and from the person of the psychoanalyst. Instead, the analyst becomes the good satisfying mother—better than all the others. Being ego-syntonic, both may enjoy that fiction.

When the analyst gets caught up with the patient through these countertransference engagements and joint enactments occur,[14] the patient may be acutely aware of what is happening to the analyst.[15] Three possibilities then arise: (a) the patient *incorrectly* sees his phantasies in the analyst; (b) the patient *correctly* sees his phantasies in the analyst's state of mind and behaviour; and (c) the patient is instrumental to some degree in creating his own phantasies of the analyst's mind (a role-responsiveness—Sandler, 1976). In any of these cases, from the patient's point of view, he is in relation to a mind that is in some respects disturbed.

There is a tendency that, the more disturbed the patient, the more acutely they scan the analyst's interpretations to assess what is happening to the analyst's mind. Interpretations that for the analyst are insights generously offered are for the patient quite different. They may seem like openings into the working of the analyst's mind that tell the patient if he has done damage or not, and, maybe, give evidence to the patient of the analyst's resentment or retaliation—or forgiveness.

Object-relational "play"

In the British psychoanalytical tradition a second main source of ideas on countertransference came from Ferenczi's clinical experimentation (1988). This was continued by Balint in Budapest and brought to London in the 1930s (Balint & Balint, 1939; Balint, 1950). This "Ferenczi tradition" has been represented by the British Independent group of analysts (Kohon, 1986; Rayner, 1991; Stewart, 1996).

Ferenczi's experiments, which he bravely recorded in his *Clinical Diary* (1988), seemed to assume that knowledge would operate one way only. Only the patient is known. And that was in line with the requirement for a blank-screen analyst. However, in the interests of equality (and for attacking regression), he arranged the setting such that it could be reversed. Whereas, normally, the analyst is in a position to know the patient, reversing the physical position of analyst and patient would reverse who gets to know whom. Balint (1936) reviewed Ferenczi's experiments, recommending, ultimately, that the classical technique should be adhered to in most cases. Little (1951), however, examined this question, too, and recommended that the analyst occasionally share her analysis of her own feelings with the patient.

Balint stressed that *both* the patient and the analyst have libidinal investments in each other and in the analysis. But, he also suggested, the understanding of the patient's transference and of the analyst's countertransference do not exhaust the necessary work. Descriptions of the states of the two individuals "remain incomplete through the neglect of an essential feature, namely, that all these phenomena happen in an inter-relation between two individuals, in a constantly changing and developing object-relation" (1950, p. 123).

That object relation is the "interplay of transference and counter-transference" (p. 123) and forms something superordinate. Balint stressed the "creating [of] a proper atmosphere for the patient by the analyst" (p. 123), and asserted that each analyst is unique and contributes his own atmosphere to the particular analysis.

This is echoed in Winnicott's injunction "to avoid breaking up this natural process by making interpretations" (Winnicott, 1969, p. 711). Winnicott increasingly saw the transference/countertransference as a delicate arena of its own, co-constructed by both parties. Making interpretations interrupts a natural process. "I think I interpret mainly to let the patient know the limits of my understanding. The principle is that it is the patient and only the patient who has the answers" (p. 711).

These are founding statements of a trend, characteristic of the British Independents, which address the relationship in a holistic manner rather than picking off the individuals separately. Winnicott came to theorise that trend most notably with his descriptions of a third area, the transitional space, which he specified as having the qualities of both "me" and "not-me" at the same time. This is the area in which the person can continue to "indulge in a play" that gratifies their infantile omnipotence into adult life (Winnicott, 1971). At its extreme, the notion of countertransference has been absorbed simply into a consideration of personal style that collaborates with the patient's.[16] The origins with Ferenczi's experiments have led many object-relations analysts to refute the suggestion that analysts might share their feelings with their patients that Bollas (1989) has discussed at some length. Nevertheless, the recognition that the analyst's style and the atmosphere engendered become a playful creativity between patient and analyst has developed strong roots in the Independent tradition. It appears to offer the patient an equal partnership in a process that restores a normal mutuality in the "affective response" of one to the other.

When this mutuality seems to be interrupted, the analyst will, modestly, tend to assume that the patient feels the analyst has missed something in what the patient is expressing. The Independent analyst will then engage in an internal supervision (Casement, 1985).

These notions of creative play, or of the analyst's failed receptivity requiring self-supervision, are probably comparable to Money-Kyrle's notion of normal and deviant phases of countertransference. However, these positions are theorised quite differently. And they lead to technical differences.

Klein/Independent comparisons

These two main strands of the object-relations tradition (the Independents and the Klein Group) differ primarily over the way they attend to the "space" between analyst and patient. In particular, Kleinians address this interpersonal space as one to be analysed in intrapsychic terms. Independent object-relations analysts will regard it as a separate space between, in which both can invent and practise a creative, spontaneous relating. This leads also to different views about action in the psychoanalytic setting.

While becoming embroiled in the affects, the analyst aims to become aware of this, and to recognise the relationships that the patient is seeking out. The question is how much to refrain from going along with these proffered relationships—or actively to manipulate new ones. We need to distinguish between *recognising* this demanded role and *performing* it.

To a degree, the patient will want it recognised, and thus wants the analyst's mind to recognise him in this way. In part, he will seek to understand himself. Bion's formulation of the relational links is useful here. He postulated a specific epistemophilic link, based on Klein's work on curiosity and the epistemophilic impulse; and he called this a "K"-link (1962). He contrasted it with the more familiar emotional links that he characterised as "L" (loving and being loved), and "H" (hating and being hated). The "K"-link is the specific relationship of knowing and being known, and represents the enquiry and curiosity about another's mind.

Engaging in the "L"- and "H"-links amounts to emotional gratification, which Freud's rule of abstinence proscribes. In Bion's terms (1967), Freud's abstinence is in order to prioritise the "K"-link, and to maximise the conditions for it. In other words, whatever kind of "mating" the patient seeks with whatever part of the analyst's mind, the analyst, in role, seeks to mate with the patient in a "K"-link.

In the different schools there is a diverging identity of what the analyst is. One view depends on Klein's discoveries that lead to the attempt to sustain an identity founded on epistemophilia and therefore an identity in the "K"-link. The other, rooted in Balint's development of Ferenczi, and melded with Winnicott's rejection of Klein, seeks a flexible analytic identity negotiated with the patient to create and practise new relationships.

So these theoretical considerations lead to some sharp divergences in technical practice, between the Kleinian tradition and the British Independents', or "Ferenczi" tradition.

1) Kleinians use the analyst's feelings as a source of material to be analysed as an indication of the enactments they have become embroiled in—a complement to the patient's free associations. For Independents, their feelings are an important factor (maybe *the* important factor) in creating a therapeutic ambience to the setting.

2) This difference rests, partly, on the Kleinian emphasis on the epistemic goal of analysis—to know what is happening. In contrast, the Independents aim for a joint or mutual creativity within the "in-between" of the affective relationship. The Independents' goal is a new, different relationship, rather than new insight.

3) Clearly assigned roles enacted between two partners in a Kleinian analysis reflect their theoretical assumption of a clear ego boundary at birth; while to many in the Independent group the mutual constructions of play in the analytic setting will correspond to an initial post-natal phase of a merged, infantile phase of omnipotence.[17]

4) Finally, this leads to a contrast in the view of enactment. For Kleinians, the analyst's unconscious enactments with the patient may be informative; but only so if raised to conscious awareness—and it therefore attracts a negative evaluation. On the other hand, a view of a joint creative moment between the two merged partners allows the potential for "positive" forms of enactment in the Independent view.

In general, countertransference retains the quality of a pathology about it in the Kleinian tradition—albeit a pathology with potential for being turned into a powerful source of new knowledge about the specific pathology. In the Independent "Ferenczi tradition", however, countertransference has an added value. It offers a field for the patient to acquire, with the analyst, experience of true interpersonal creativity.

Ego-psychology

Ego-psychologists have adhered to Freud's notion of counter-transference as simply interference,[18] and written relatively little on the topic. For example, classical texts such as Hartmann (1964) or Rapaport (1967) do not index the term. And, indeed, in looking at recent developments, Eagle (1984) does not index it either.

Hartmann and Rapaport put their emphasis firmly on the ego's management of drive-reduction, the clearing of libido out of the system. Their theories were a product of creatively grafting Freud's energic model upon the structural model. Analysis of the analyst was then the straightforward answer to countertransference. He should be able, as it were by conscious determination, to detach himself from his experiences.

> [The analyst's] mental attitude during his work, the freely hovering attention from which he starts off first into understanding and then into communication, has an unmistakable correlation to the ability to control regression. In his own affective reaction he is limited to the affect signal, and its use—sometimes confused with counter-transference—becomes an important tool. The ability to detach himself from his own experience, the step from self-observation to self-analysis, remains his constant companion. [E. Kris, 1956, p. 453]

A kind of objective self-detached recognition of the "affect-signal" should bring into play a detached function of self-observation. Any trend in the analyst towards more immediate drive-reduction satisfactions can in principle be eradicated with enough good psychoanalysis of the analyst's personality.

This description of the rule of abstinence largely preserves the "blank screen" notion of analytic technique—the supposed detachment from personal experience. Ego-psychologists based this argument on the separation within the ego of certain autonomous functions (Hartmann, 1939). These functions are not subject to the neurotic conflicts of the Oedipus complex. A psychoanalyst's business is to extend the patient's autonomous conflict-free sphere of operation. This is the ego-psychology interpretation of "where id is, there shall ego be". This, the analyst must achieve, too, in his work. Thus, analytic functioning and interpretation according to ego-psychologists proceed from the conflict-free sphere of ego activity—or they should do.

Critical comparisons

There are major differences between the object-relations viewpoints and that of ego-psychology. Applying the energy model to the structural model contrasts with Klein, who took the structural model as liberating psychoanalysis from the physics of the libido.

1) Drive reduction is the first aim of the mental apparatus according to ego-psychology, rather than the stronger emphasis on conflict resolution in Klein.
2) In Kleinian and object-relations approaches, the ego is subjected to potential conflicts in all areas of function. The conflict-free autonomous areas of ego-psychology do not exist and that applies to the ego of the analyst. Countertransference is therefore seen as inevitable, something to be made the best of.
3) Therefore countertransference is a hindrance to conflict-free functioning according to ego-psychology, while it is a sensitive detector in Kleinian and many object-relations theories.

Contemporary Freudians of London

The group of British analysts who were students of Anna Freud were, for a long time, identified with the ego-psychologists of North America. More recently they have made theoretical moves to bridge the gap between themselves and British object relations—especially Kleinian ideas.

They have been particularly influenced by the notion of projective identification as a significant element in countertransference.[19] Sandler (1993) noted that the development of more and more schools of psychoanalytic theory increases interest in clinical practice, clinical material and the theory of psychoanalytic practice.

In that paper, he refers to a reflex form of identification in which all people will primitively empathise with (or really, imitate) others" emotions and even predicaments. This he has said has different names according to who has described it: "primitive passive sympathy" McDougall (1909); "primary identification" (Freud, 1923); "resonance duplication" (Weiss, 1960), or Sandler's preferred term "recurrent primary identification".

This "echo" of the patient's feelings and behaviour in the analyst has been very influential in Sandler's thinking about transference–countertransference interactions. The analyst is subjected, whether he wants to be or not, to a pressure to respond to the emotional content of the patient. Sandler used this idea of "empathic" listening to consider the Kleinian notion of the countertransference enactment. Sandler (1976) preferred to call it a "role-responsive-ness". In this, Sandler described the role that the patient is expecting to find in the analyst, and one that is, in fact, actualised in the analyst's experiences and maybe behaviour.

Sandler has seemed to prefer to keep the term countertransference to refer to the original neurotic conception of the term. For the more recent expansion he then retains the term "role-responsive-ness" of the analyst or sometimes "role-actualisation".

The closeness of Sandler's thinking to Kleinian perceptions of the clinical occurrences has led Kleinians more recently to recognise the equivalence of Sandler's terms with theirs (for instance, O'Shaughnessy, 1992, Feldman, 1993). Together with this degree of convergence with Kleinian views on the analytic relationship, Sandler's terminology has become increasingly used within North American ego-psychology and its derivatives, especially those analysts with an intersubjectivist position (for instance Renik, 1993; Ogden, 1994).

The intersubjectivists have also influenced the London group, perhaps especially Fonagy's (1991; Target & Fonagy, 1996) theory of mentalisation: "I would like to label the capacity to conceive of conscious and unconscious mental states in oneself and others as the capacity to *mentalize*" (Fonagy, 1991, p. 641). Fonagy's point is that at a particular point in the maturation of infants there comes a realisation that a mind exists in other, external objects comparable with its capacity to feel its own experiences. This step is a crucial one in the infant entering the psychological world, and marks the beginning of a psychological mindedness that he calls "mentalisa-tion". Mentalisation is the regard for the interiority and subjectivity of the object that is therefore not merely exploited for purposes of drive reduction, but is related to another subject. This indicates the infant's dawning awareness of other people who have minds too, a problem that Fonagy says adult borderline personalities are still struggling with. It is a conception that clearly overlaps with the Kleinian "depressive position", a conception that has gained wide influence in British psychoanalysis and thus influenced Fonagy (see Mitrani, 1993 for a Kleinian sense of the term "mentalise"). The recognition by the patient of the analyst's mind as a key element in the patient's external reality points towards the present Kleinian interest in the countertransference, and analyst-centred interpretations.

Kleinians might disagree about the point at which this mentalisation step occurs, since a Kleinian view would have it that there is a potential idea of a mind within the object from very early on and probably at birth (an innate preconception). But that disagreement is at a theoretical level. As Sandler says, we could see the level of clinical work as a new driving force that is affecting a rapprochement between Kleinian views and those of the classical Freudians in London and also some ego-psychologists, particularly the intersubjectivists. However, on the whole these overtures towards a Kleinian terminology in which the subject of the patient becomes a feature of psychoanalysis distance the London con-temporary Freudians somewhat from ego-psychology. These developments follow on from reservations about classical ego-psychology, reservations that parallel those of self-psychologists and interpersonalists, to which we will now briefly turn.

Escape from ego-psychology

The meticulous application of the energy model and the dominance of theoretical precision over clinical observation led to an increas-ingly mechanistic "feel" about the practice—or at least the reporting—of ego-psychologists' work. So, this fundamentally mechanistic stance seems in recent times to have run out of steam!

Some North American analysts did express an early dissenting voice from the drive-reduction model: for instance Searles (1959a, b) and Kernberg (1965). Escape from ego-psychology comes in part from the pressure of the new views on countertransference that developed outside ego-psychology (especially in the object-relations traditions) in the 1950s and 1960s (Wolstein, 1983). The development of ego-psychology theory carried the analyst too far from the patient's experience (Kohut, 1982).

From the mid-1970s new theoretical frameworks have re-examined countertransference (Peterfreund, 1975; Langs, 1976; G. Klein, 1976; Schafer, 1976). These moves away from the high point of ego-psychology have tended to bring in, and give more emphasis to, relational or communicative aspects of the psychoanalytic setting. From the vantage point of the present, two trends seem to emerge: first, self-psychology and, second, the intersubjectivists.

Self-psychology

Deliberately moving away from ego-psychology, Kohut (1971) inserted a suffering self as a ghost in the machine. Self-psychology, with the purpose of adding the relationship with the self to classic psychoanalysis, continued to regard countertransference as neurotic interference. This interference[20] disturbs the calm of a stance devoted centrally to empathic listening and providing the experience of a mirror to the patient's narcissism. That countertransference mirror may do two things: it either constitutes (a) the self, by replaying a self-observing function for the patient; or (b) an opportunity for a grandiose fusion with an object perceived as ideal. Such a mirror needs a high degree of polish and freedom from contaminants, and the analyst might introduce those in the form of his own neurotic countertransference.

Self-psychology has thereby taken a new view of the non-transferential aspect of the analyst's experience. While the patient may be divided between the transference and the therapeutic alliance (the conflict-free aspect of the ego), the analyst's contrasting aspects are the countertransference (neurotic) and empathy. In particular the analyst's empathy confronts the patient's narcissistic self. In self-psychology that confrontation, perhaps on its own, is curative. This leads to a more open, interactive style of work, and one that is less devoted to insight and more to corrective experiences based on the analyst's empathy (Bacal, 1990).

Critical comparisons

There are clear points of comparison between empathy and the notion of countertransference as understood in other schools of psychoanalysis.

1) The experience of the self emerges through the other's *experience*, not just through his knowledge. This gives the countertransference a peculiar priority in cure. Psychoanalysis gives expression to something unexpressed and inexpressible in the interaction between transference and countertransference—not just to something formulated but unconscious. In this creative way the experiences of both patient and analyst approach the conceptions of the British Independents.
2) Environmental deficit is given a supreme position over conflict, and the implications for countertransference are that a non-conflicted empathy is a necessary and perhaps sufficient provision (or re-provision) for cure in the analytic setting.
3) The notion of a mirror experience is explicit also in the developmental psychologies of both Winnicott and Lacan. The mirror-role for the analyst is termed by Kohut the mirror transference. Like Winnicott, Kohut regarded this as a benevolent (perhaps an all-good) experience for the patient in developing his self-identity. Lacan on the other hand regards this as a necessary but malignant imposition of society upon the unformed infant.

Intersubjectivists

Certain other psychoanalysts have effected a different solution to the same problems of ego-psychology—its mechanisation. These recent inheritors of the ego-psychology tradition share with self-psychologists their emphasis on the subject—the subjectivity of the patient and of the analyst. The increasing (perhaps democratising) pressures of society towards an equality in the relationship between patient and analyst have influenced the conception of a mutuality between the partners.[21] Their concern was that ego-psychology failed to investigate how the observer affects the observed in psychoanalysis (Atwood & Stolorow, 1984; Stolorow *et al.*, 1987).

Indeed at times they seem to draw from the Independent tradition in Britain; although at other times (or with other people) they turn equally towards the primitive mechanisms stressed by Kleinians (Ogden, 1994).

Ogden's "intersubjective resonance of unconscious processes of individuals experiencing one another as subjects" (1988, p. 23) described a specific framework for thinking how the patient and analyst, as interdependent subject and object (transference and countertransference) come together to form a "third object"—or the jointly created analytic third (Ogden, 1994). The analyst's experience, termed the countertransference in its broadest sense, contributes a body of "intersubjective" clinical facts. He may experience them as the apparently self-absorbed ramblings of his mind, bodily sensations that seemingly have nothing to do with the analysand, or any other intersubjectively generated phenomenon within the analytic pair (Ogden, 1994).

The therapeutic stress is placed on the view that individual subjectivity is within the intersubjective context. This has brought back a re-examination of Sullivan and the long tradition of interpersonal psychoanalysis (Levenson, 1984; Cushman, 1994). However, the therapeutic focus of the intersubjectivists is on the psychoanalytic context, the patient's context being the interacting analyst—and this contrasts with the approach of the interpersonalists that emphasised the social contexts outside the analysis. Their focus of interpretation on the here-and-now also brings these analysts close to all forms of the British schools.

Critical comparisons

The Intersubjectivists are varied in their own right, but certain aspects of their approach contrast with the adjacent schools of interpersonalists and of the British object-relations schools.

1) Many of the intersubjectivists rest heavily on the Kleinian notion of projective identification for their exploration of interpersonal space, but on the whole they repudiate the role of destructiveness in the Kleinian concept.

2) Intersubjectivists tend to discount extra-transference, extra-relational material, in favour of the mutually created moment,

which contrasts with Klein's use of the transference as the "total situation".

3) The Intersubjectivists move away from the notion of the sealed unit of the person characteristic of individual psychology, which is the focus for most of the psychoanalytic practice of most schools.

4) The Intersubjectivists differ from interpersonal psychoanalysis by stressing the therapeutic here-and-now (as in British psycho-analysis), not the reach for the social context as did Sullivan.

5) The Intersubjectivists draw back from the self-psychologists' postulate of a relationship with the self, in the form of a self-object.

Lacan

Lacan's technique is highly eccentric in relation to other schools of psychoanalysis. Transference and countertransference are equally suspect. Relations with others in the interpersonal field mean the imposition of the social upon the individual. Lacan like others thought that ego-psychology was deeply out of sympathy with the essentials in psychoanalysis. Lacan's interpersonal stance has something in common with the Intersubjectivists. However, Lacan's theoretical constructions are different. Lacan took a politically radical stance. He described the socialisation of the infant as the imposition of the structured symbolic world of society upon a seemingly pristine naïveté. He describes this as the clash between the imaginary order and the symbolic order, enforced most strongly by language. In Lacan's view this is replayed as a power struggle within the psychoanalysis. As in infancy, the analyst (parent) always "wins".

Limentani (1986), in his presidential address to the IPA quoted Donnet's (1979) comparison of the psychoanalytic framework with the maternal body. He also quoted Donnet's footnote:

He reports in a footnote as follows: "An analysand of Lacan as he lies down begins: 'At last' ... 'Good', said Lacan, terminating the session." Of course, anyone can see that there is something highly stimulating, provocative and capable of mobilizing a lot of heat in response to such behaviour on the part of the analyst, but what has this got to do with psychoanalysis? Is it worth discussing? We all know that we are not too sure of our reasons for fixing the duration of the sessions at 45 or 50 minutes. [1986, p. 236]

Lacan's service to psychoanalysis may be more to stimulate thinking about the rigid doctrines that pass as psychoanalytic theory (Spero, 1993). As Spero commented, the unfixed and unpredictable ending of a session, is only so from one point of view, but has a natural evolution in another view. Giving an interpretation also has the same unexpected and unfixed qualities, from the patient's point of view. That punctuation of the hour by interpretation is accepted by mainstream analysts, largely without thinking. Lacan's questions about the experience of time, prompted by the duration of the session, point towards a wider need to theorise the setting. Spero concluded that "the temporal pattern of the hour [is] an integral ego function implicit in the analytic envelope" (1993, p. 139).

The infant is aware of himself only as he becomes aware of others, or specifically as he becomes aware of others' awareness of him. Lacan called this the mirror stage (1949). The infant thus knows himself only as he is perceived and structured by the perception of others. In the psychoanalytic work the same applies. The patient increases his knowledge of himself only through the structured knowledge of his analyst.

Lacan dispensed with the term "countertransference" (1966) on the grounds that it conveyed a reciprocity between the patient gripped by transference and the analyst by countertransference, but this relationship is far from equal (Lacan, 1977; Aslan, 1989). Lacan was concerned with the "desire" of the analyst as much as the desires of the patient. Both patient and analyst have desires of the analysis.[22] The patient's desires clearly include those of a primitive transference kind; he desires to be the object of the analyst's desire. But the analyst too has desires. At the very least he desires to be a good analyst, to cure the patent, and maybe to advance psycho-analysis itself. In his own formation he is socially required to be the "one who is supposed to know" (le sujet-supposé-savoir—Lacan, 1949). This implies a destructive negotiation over possession of the knowledge of the patient. Lacan (1991) took Money-Kyrle's (1956) clinical illustration of countertransference to convey the kind of unconscious jousting that may occur (see Palomera, 1997).

In this sense, the patient is the focus of the analyst's satisfaction of his desire. And the analyst is in a privileged position in this regard, potentially to achieve his own satisfaction. The patient is therefore alienated from himself as the analyst's object of desire.

Lacan derived his view of countertransference from the classical Freudian position—that it is interference, and something that interferes directly in the patient (Lacan, 1951; Muller & Richardson, 1982). As Etchegoyen wrote, "the transference begins when the countertransference destroys the development of the dialectic process" (1991, p. 297). However, Lacan rejected the classical Freudian principle of technical neutrality (Evans, 1996). Like Heimann he accepted that the analyst has his own reactions and these interfere with the patient in important ways. However, Lacan believed that an analyst's own analysis only made his desire more apparent and overt. Technically instead Lacan believes the formation of the analyst in the symbolic order is that the analyst adopts a new desire, "the desire of the analyst". That should be a kind of anti-desire, a desire not to desire cure etc., not to impose upon the patient. This paradox seems to emerge too in the apparent contradiction of Lacan's orthodox wish to avoid the imposition of his powerful position as the object of transference (desire), when, at the same time, he imposes an entirely arbitrary time-span on the analytic session that is totally in the hands of the analyst (Spero, 1993).[23]

Critical comparisons

Despite Lacan's arcane language of puns and confusions, many of his preoccupations resemble those of mainstream psychoanalysts, although he has the ability to turn these on their head in bizarre ways.

1) Lacan's view of the modifications of the patient's unformulated experiences by the analyst recall Bion's instruction to abandon memory and desire. A number of writers have noted this correspondence (for instance, Aslan, 1989; Bader, 1994; Barratt, 1994).[24] Bion's idea of containing, however, allows the potential for a creative outcome, as well as the possibility of a nameless dread; for Lacan only the latter is anticipated.

2) The social presence of the person in the symbolic world of language is only persecutory. Thus culture is psychoanalytically ambiguous, civilisation the source of discontent, and verbal interpretations the weapons of domination.
3) Winnicott (1967) accepted Lacan's view of the role of the "other" as a defining mirror for the child. Like Lacan, Winnicott would claim this is a necessary phase and function of the object. In contrast to Lacan's formulation, Winnicott stresses its uncomplicated benign quality.
4) Lacan's suspicion of imposed aspects of character, and thus faulty self-recognition (Grotstein, 1994), has a strong resemblance to Winnicott's "false self" experience.
5) Lacan's cognitive emphasis contrasts his style with those of most mainstream analysts where emotions are the energic powerhouse of desires or of relationships, and the focus of interpretation.

Lacan's suspicion of the vulnerability of individuals to distortion by the power position of the analyst almost rules out any professional activity at all.

Conclusion

All views on countertransference that have developed during the last fifty years have embraced the realisation that the analyst's identity includes a feeling person. He has a personal identity as well as a professional identity, and both are implicated in work that goes wrong, and that which goes right as well. This increasing mutuality is the psychoanalytic response to the rhetoric in society at large demanding a democratisation of professional identity. That pressure strikes a chord in the notion of countertransference, the most personal of all professional tools.

Many schools are now embracing the realisation that the analyst's identity includes a feeling person. But what person is that?

The role he experiences in the countertransference is not just a matter of professional competence, it is also one of personal identity: what conscious and unconscious role is he entering into with his patient? He strives to be an analyst; yet he plays a part in his patient's phan-tasies; and, in addition, he has his own conscious and unconscious phantasy life that he plays out with his objects.

The externalisation of the psychic world of the patient, therapeutically amplified, into the transference, leads to a number of possible ways of seeing the intrapsychic pattern of the counter-transference: (a) the patient may *incorrectly* see the analyst as a character in his phantasies; or (b) the analyst's state of mind may, for serendipitous reasons, accord with the patient's phantasies, or (c), finally, the patient in fact provokes the analyst into responding "in role". From the patient's point of view all these occurrences are equivalent since he retains a belief in the analyst being the character that exists as an internal object.

But another possibility exists. This, espoused by the Independents and the Intersubjectivists, has an interpersonal focus. It is that both partners may contribute to a common creation between them. This transitional space, or analytic third, has a strongly optimistic thrust. It contrasts with the strongly negative connotations put on the intrusion of the analyst into this space, described by Lacan. Both Balint and Lacan have stressed the impinging needs of the analyst as well as of the patient.

From a Kleinian point of view the risk is of impinging into the patient's intrapsychic world. For Kleinians, action upon another person or upon their mind is attributable to a violent form of object-relating or to a mutant (non-verbal) form of communication. Redemption is to bring these under a verbal conscious enquiry or scrutiny. This leads to some divergence from other schools where the emphasis is on keeping the correct balance between play and impingement, or for the self-psychologists a pristine, and un-clouded, mirror of the patient.

This paper has been an account of divergences from the vantage point of one of them. The distortions and inaccuracies I have introduced may be, to a major extent, my own limitations, but to a degree they will also point to particular preoccupations and restrictions in a specifically Kleinian viewpoint.

Countertransference has become a useful nodal point for grasping the divergences between psychoanalytic schools. As it is a debate about the personal identity of each psychoanalyst as he works as a professional, these divergences follow through into the wide diversity of technical practices between the schools, and indeed between individual analysts. Increasingly, psychoanalysis has accepted that the personal is professional.

Acknowledgements

I am grateful to my colleague Joan Raphael-Leff for her encouragement and advice in writing parts of this paper. And to Richard Rusbridger and Bob Michels for comments on earlier drafts.

Notes

1. That research project was in fact presaged by Freud: "It is a very remarkable thing that the Ucs. of one human being can react upon that of another, without passing through the Cs. This deserves closer investigation" (Freud, 1915, p. 194).
2. According to the PEP Archive CD-ROM only 90 articles referred to countertransference prior to 1950 (1.6% of all articles), whereas from 1950 onwards there were 3,685 such articles (16.5% of all articles).
3. We can also find early references in Jung (1929) to countertransference as a highly important organ of communication.
4. See also his "The psychology of the psychotherapist" (Glover, 1928).
5. Melanie Klein had already made significant developments in widening the understanding of transference to include the notion that all aspects of the patient's association addressed some part of the transference however remote, unconscious or split-off (Klein, 1943, 1952; Joseph, 1985).
6. Significantly, they were originally (in the 1920s) called "control analyses", and consisted largely of discussions of the analysand's difficulties arising in the training cases under supervision.
7. "The mind ... achieves adaptation and progress by employing throughout its existence the fundamental and basic processes of introjection and projection. Consequently, the mechanism of taking in and expelling, or if we think of their psychical correlates, introjecting and projecting are vital processes of the first magnitude ... Such taking in and expelling consists of an active interplay between the organism and the outer world; on this fundamental pattern rests all intercourse between subject and object ... in the last analysis we may find it at the bottom of all our complicated dealings with one another" (Heimann, 1943, p. 507).
8. The frozen reaction is akin to the blank screen, which may in effect be a rationalised defence against emotional reactions.
9. In her early paper on countertransference (1951), Margaret Little recognised the *effect* on the patient of an analyst's countertransference feelings. She stressed the importance of the phobic reaction to the

patient's feelings—which leads to what Brenman Pick called freezing.

10. To a degree Kleinian interpretation has tended to change from the former to the latter. Spillius (1988) has also noted a significant change in contemporary Kleinian technique over the last two decades or so.

11. Sometimes, Kleinian technique has been regarded as *actually* blaming the patient for intruding via projective identification. Indeed, there is also the issue of the analyst feeling burdened with blame and guilt, and this may lead the analyst to become defensive, or to use the patient to confess to. The analyst's feelings of blame are an important but little discussed aspect of countertransference that can lead to stressful relations between analysts themselves.

12. Sandler (1976) has used the terms "role actualisation" or "role-responsiveness" when the analyst does adopt the required role.

13. Of course the analyst needs some confirmation from the content of the material that the analyst's feelings mean something in the patient's terms, and probably the reverse is true as well.

14. Enactments are thus a part of the patient's defensive system, or, in Freud's terms, the transference cure.

15. And this occurred, for instance, with the patient that Money-Kyrle described (1956).

16. This is a required spontaneity, as it were. And no doubt it is aimed at counteracting the freezing process described earlier, associated with the blank screen.

17. However, Raphael-Leff (1993), for instance, has stressed that many analysts have had to take account of the recent experimental psychology research on babies with their mothers, and are moving away from the notion of a primary merging, and describe a primary form of mutual play between mothers and infants.

18. For instance, as late as 1994, Anton Kris reviewed the problems of countertransference in these terms in Joan Riviere's analysis with Jones and Freud.

19. Anna Freud's notion of "identification with the aggressor" points to a correspondence with Klein's notion of projective identification.

20. Some self-psychologists may subsequently have modified this "negative" view of countertransference (see Orange, 1993).

21. I have, probably inaccurately and unfairly, conflated the long tradition of the interpersonalist analysts since Harry Stack Sullivan, Erich Fromm and Clara Thompson into this more recent intersubjective trend. I believe I do not give sufficient regard to the differences (Levenson, 1984; Wolstein, 1983). Nevertheless, for want of space (and also direct acquaintance) I am constrained in this way.

22. When Elizabeth Zetzel went before the Admissions Committee of the

74   KEY PAPERS ON COUNTERTRANSFERENCE

London Psychoanalytic Institute, Ernest Jones told her: "Whatever you do, don't tell them that you want to help the patient". Told by Zetzel at a panel of the American Psychoanalytic Association (Zabarenko, 1993).
23. Lacan's suspicion of the regimenting effect of words and language make it thoroughly ironic that he ever became interested in the *talking* cure.
24. The comparison has been particularly noted by those South Americans who long ago espoused European ideas in advance of North American ones (for instance Baranger, 1993; Azevedo, 1994).

References

Aslan, C. M. (1989). Common ground in psychoanalysis: aims and clinical process. As I see it. *Int. J. Psychoanal.*, 70: 12–16.

Atwood, G., & Stolorow, R. (1984). *Structures of Subjectivity: Explorations in Psychoanalytic Phenomenology.* Hillsdale, NJ: Analytic Press.

Azevedo, A. M. A. de (1994). Validation of the psychoanalytic clinical process: the role of dreams. *Int. J. Psychoanal.*, 75: 1181–1192.

Bacal, H. (1990). Does an object relations theory exist in self psychology? *Psychoanal. Inq.*, 9: 197–220.

Bader, M. (1994). The tendency to neglect therapeutic aims in psycho-analysis. *Psychoanal. Q.*, 63: 246–270.

Balint, A. (1936). Handhabung der Übertragung auf Grund der Ferenczischen Versuche. *Int. Zeit. Psychoanal.*, 22.

Balint, M. (1936). The final goal of psycho-analytic treatment. *Int. J. Psychoanal.*, 17: 206–216.

Balint, M. (1950). Changing therapeutical aims and techniques in psycho-analysis. *Int. J. Psychoanal.*, 31: 117–124.

Balint, M., & Balint, A. (1939). On transference and counter-transference. *Int. J. Psychoanal.*, 20: 223–230.

Baranger, M. (1993). The mind of the analyst: from listening to interpretation. *Int. J. Psychoanal.*, 74: 15–24.

Barratt, B. (1994). Critical notes on the psychoanalyst's theorising. *J. Amer. Psychoanal. Assn.*, 42: 697–725.

Bion, W. R. (1961). *Experiences in Groups.* London: Tavistock.

Bion, W. R. (1959). Attacks on linking. *Int. J. Psycho-anal.*, 40: 308–315.

Bion, W. R. (1962). *Learning from Experience.* London: Heinemann.

Bion, W. R. (1967). Notes on memory and desire. *Psycho-anal. Forum*, 2: 272–273.

Bollas, C. (1989). *Forces of Destiny: Psychoanalysis and Human Idiom.* London: Free Association Books.

Brenman Pick, I. (1985). Working through in the countertransference. *Int. J. Psychoanal., 66*: 157–166.

Casement, P. (1985). *Learning from the Patient.* London: Tavistock.

Cushman, P. (1994). Confronting Sullivan's spider—hermeneutics and the politics of therapy. *Contemp. Psychoanal., 30*: 800–844.

Donnet, J.-L. (1979). Sur l'institution psychanalytique et la durée de la séance. *Nouv. Rev. Psychoanal., 20*: 242–259.

Eagle, M. (1984). *Recent Developments in Psychoanalysis.* New York: McGraw-Hill.

Etchegoyen, H. (1991). *The Fundamentals of Psychoanalytic Technique.* London: Karnac.

Evans, D. (1996). *Dictionary of Lacanian Psychoanalysis.* London: Routledge.

Feldman, M. (1993). The dynamics of reassurance. *Int. J. Psychoanal., 74*: 275–285.

Feldman, M. (1997). Projective identification: the analyst's involvement. *Int. J. Psychoanal., 78*: 227–241.

Feldman, M., & Spillius, E. (1989). Introduction to Part 2. In: Betty Joseph (Ed.), *Psychic Equilibrium and Psychic Change.* London: Routledge.

Fenichel O. (1941). On transference and counter-transference. *Psychoanal. Q., 10*: 682–683.

Fenichel O. (1979). Problems of psychoanalytic technique. *Psychoanal. Q., 8*: 164–185.

Ferenczi, S. (1988). *The Clinical Diary of Sándor Ferenczi.* Cambridge, MA: Harvard Univ. Press.

Fonagy, P. (1991). Thinking about thinking: some clinical and theoretical considerations in the treatment of a borderline patient. *Int. J. Psycho-anal., 72*: 639–656.

Freud, S. (1909). *Five Lectures on Psycho-Analysis. S.E., 11.*

Freud, S. (1912). Recommendations to physicians practising psychoanalysis. *S.E., 12.*

Freud, S. (1915). The unconscious. *S.E., 14.*

Freud, S. (1923). *The Ego and the Id. S.E., 19.*

Gitelson, M. (1952). The emotional response of the analyst in the psychoanalytic situation. *Int. J. Psychoanal., 33*: 1–10.

Glover, E. (1927). Lectures on technique in psycho-analysis. *Int. J. Psychoanal., 8*: 486–520.

Glover, E. (1928). The psychology of the psychotherapist. *Brit. J. Med. Psychol.*, *9*: 1–16.

Grotstein, J. (1994). Projective identification and countertransference: a brief commentary on their relationship. *Contemp. Psychoanal.*, *30*: 578–592.

Hartmann, H. (1939). Ego psychology and the problem of adaptation. In: D. Rapaport (Ed.), *Organization and Pathology of Thought* (pp. 362–396). New York: Columbia Univ. Press.

Hartmann, H. (1964). *Essays in Ego-Psychology*. New York: Int. Univ. Press.

Heimann, P. (1943). Some aspects of the role of introjection and projection in early development. In: P. King & R. Steiner (Eds.), *The Freud–Klein Controversies 1941–1945* (pp. 501–530). London: Routledge, 1991.

Heimann, P. (1950). On counter-transference. *Int. J. Psychoanal.*, *31*: 81–84.

Hinshelwood, R. D. (1985). The patient's defensive analyst. *Brit. J. Psychother.*, *2*: 30–41.

Joseph, B. (1978). Different types of anxiety and their handling in the analytic situation. *Int. J. Psychoanal.*, *59*: 223–228.

Joseph, B. (1985). Transference: the total situation. *Int. J. Psychoanal.*, *66*: 447–454.

Jung, C. (1929). Problems of modern psychotherapy. *C.W.*, Volume 16.

Kernberg, O. (1965). Notes on countertransference. *J. Amer. Psychoanal. Assn.*, *13*: 38–56.

King, P. (1978). Affective response of the analyst to the patient's communications. *Int. J. Psycho-anal.*, *59*: 329–334.

Klein, G. (1976). *Psychoanalytic Theory*. New York: Int. Univ. Press.

Klein, M. (1943). Memorandum on her technique. In: Pearl King & Riccardo Steiner (Eds.), *The Freud–Klein Controversies, 1941–1945* (pp. 635–638). London: Routledge, 1991.

Klein, M. (1952). The origins of transference. In: *The Writings of Melanie Klein, Volume 3* (pp. 1–24). London: Hogarth.

Kohon, G. (Ed.) (1986). *The British School of Psychoanalysis: The Independent Tradition*. London: Free Association Books.

Kohut, H. (1971). *The Analysis of the Self*. New York: Int. Univ. Press.

Kohut, H. (1982). Introspection, empathy, and the semi-circle of mental health. *Int. J. Psychoanal.*, *63*: 395–407.

Kris, A. (1994). Freud's treatment of a narcissistic patient. *Int. J. Psychoanal.*, *75*: 649–664.

Kris, E. (1956). On some vicissitudes of insight in psycho-analysis. *Int. J. Psychoanal.*, 37: 445–455.

Lacan, J. (1949). The mirror stage as formative of the function of the i as revealed in psychoanalytic experience. In: A. Sheridan (Trans.), *Écrits: A Selection* (pp. 1–7). New York: W. W. Norton & Co., 1977.

Lacan, J. (1951). Intervention sur le transfert. In: *Écrits* (pp. 215–226). Paris: Seuil, 1966.

Lacan, J. (1966). *Écrits*. Paris: Seuil.

Lacan, J. (1977). *Écrits. A Selection*. London: Routledge.

Lacan, J. (1991). *Le Séminaire, Livre VIII: Le Transfert, 1960–1961*. Paris: Seuil.

Langs, R. (1976). *The Therapeutic Interaction*. New York: Jason Aronson.

Levenson, E. A. (1984). Harry Stack Sullivan: The web and the spider. *Contemp. Psychoanal.*, 20: 174–188.

Limentani, A. (1986). Presidential address: variations on some Freudian themes. *Int. J. Psycho-anal.*, 67: 235–243.

Little, M. (1951). Counter-transference and the patient's response to it. *Int. J. Psychoanal.*, 32: 32–40.

McDougall, W. (1909). *An Introduction to Social Psychology*. London: Methuen.

Michels, R. (1997). Guest editorial. Educational section. *Int. J. Psychoanal.*, 78: 1067–1069.

Milner, M. (1952). Aspects of symbolism in comprehension of the not-self. *Int. J. Psychoanal.*, 33: 181–194.

Mitrani, J. (1993). Deficiency and envy: some factors impacting the analytic mind from listening to interpretation. *Int. J. Psychoanal.*, 74: 689–702.

Money-Kyrle, R. (1956). Normal counter-transference and some of its deviations. *Int. J. Psychoanal.*, 37: 360–366.

Muller, J., & Richardson, W. (1982). *Lacan and Language*. New York: Int. Univ. Press.

Ogden, T. (1988). On the dialectical structure of experience—some clinical and theoretical implications. *Contemp. Psychoanal.*, 24: 17–44.

Ogden, T. (1994). The analytic third: working with intersubjective clinical facts. *Int. J. Psychoanal.*, 75: 3–19.

Orange, D. M. (1993). Countertransference, empathy and the hermeneutical circle. In: A. Goldberg (Ed.), *The Widening Scope of Self Psychology: Progress in Self Psychology, Volume 9*. Hillsdale, NJ: Analytic Press.

O'Shaughnessy, E. (1992). Enclaves and excursions. *Int. J. Psychoanal.*, 73: 603–611.

Palomera, V. (1997). On counter-transference. In: B. Burgoyne & M. Sullivan (Eds.), *The Klein–Lacan Dialogues*. London: Rebus.

Peterfreund, E. (1975). The need for a new general theoretical frame of reference for psychoanalysis. *Psychoanal. Q., 44*: 534–549.

Racker, H. (1957). The meanings and uses of countertransference. *Psychoanal. Q., 26*: 303–356.

Rapaport, D. (1967). *Collected Papers*. New York: Basic Books.

Raphael-Leff, J. (1993). Prologue. In: Joan Raphael-Leff & Rosine Perelberg (Eds.), *Female Experience: Three Generations of British Women Psychoanalysts on Work with Women*. London: Routledge, 1997.

Rayner, E. (1991). *The Independent Mind in British Psychoanalysis*. London: Free Association Books.

Reich, A. (1951). On counter-transference. *Int. J. Psychoanal., 32*: 25–31.

Renik, O. (1993). Analytic interaction: conceptualising technique in light of the analyst's irreducible subjectivity. *Psychoanal. Q., 62*: 553–571.

Rosenfeld, H. (1987). *Impasse and Interpretation*. London: Routledge.

Sandler, J. (1976). Countertransference and role-responsiveness. *Int. Rev. Psychoanal., 3*: 43–47.

Sandler, J. (1993). On communication from patient to analyst: not everything is projective identification. *Int. J. Psychoanal., 74*: 1097–1107.

Schafer, R. (1976). *A New Language for Psychoanalysis*. New Haven, CT: Yale Univ. Press.

Searles, H. (1959a). The effort to drive the other person crazy. In: *Collected Papers on Psychoanalysis and Related Subjects*. New York: Int. Univ. Press.

Searles, H. (1959b). Oedipal love in the countertransference. *Int. J. Psychoanal., 40*: 180–190.

Segal, H. (1975). A psychoanalytic approach to the treatment of schizophrenia. In: Malcolm Lader (Ed.), *Studies of Schizophrenia* (pp. 94–97). Ashford: Headley.

Spero, M. H. (1993). The temporal framework and Lacan's concept of the unfixed psychoanalytic hour. *Psychoanal. Study Child, 48*: 115–142.

Spillius, E. (1988). *Melanie Klein Today*. London: Routledge.

Spillius, E. (1992). Clinical experiences of projective identification. In: R. Anderson (Ed.), *Clinical Lectures on Klein and Bion* (pp. 59–73). London: Routledge.

Steiner, J. (1993). *Psychic Retreats*. London: Routledge.

Stewart, H. (1996). *Michael Balint*. London: Routledge.

Stolorow, R. *et al.* (1987). *Psychoanalytic Treatment: An Intersubjective Approach*. Hillsdale, NJ: Analytic Press.

Target, M., & Fonagy, P. (1996). Playing with reality II: the development of psychic reality from a theoretical perspective. *Int. J. Psychoanal.*, 77: 459–479.

Weiss, E. (1960). *The Structure and Dynamics of the Human Mind*. New York: Grune & Stratton.

Winnicott, D. (1949). Hate in the countertransference. *Int. J. Psychoanal.*, 30: 69–74.

Winnicott, D. (1967). Mirror-role of mother and family in child development. In: Peter Lomas (Ed.), *The Predicament of the Family* (pp. 26–33). London: Hogarth Press.

Winnicott, D. (1969). The use of an object. *Int. J. Psychoanal.*, 50: 711–716.

Winnicott, D. (1971). *Playing and Reality*. London: Tavistock.

Wolstein, B. (1983). The pluralism of perspectives on countertransference. *Contemp. Psychoanal.*, 19: 506–521.

Zabarenko, L. M. (1993). Review of John Gedo, *The Biology of Clinical Encounters: Psychoanalysis as a Science of Mind*. In: *Psychoanalytic Books: A Quarterly Journal of Reviews*, 4: 33–39.

3: The countertransference: a Latin American view

BEATRIZ DE LEÓN DE BERNARDI, Montevideo, Uruguay

I shall be examining the concept of countertransference in the thought of Heinrich Racker and of Madeleine and Willy Baranger. Between the end of the 1940s and throughout the 1950s and 1960s, both Racker and the Barangers, working in Argentina and Uruguay, raised issues that continue to stimulate psychoanalytic reflection to this day. In this sense, these authors may be regarded as ahead of their time.

Even if my choice of subject results partly from the influence of my own training in the Uruguayan Psychoanalytic Association, which is geographically and culturally very close to Argentine psychoanalysis, I believe that these authors have been an essential, albeit in some cases controversial, reference point in the vicissitudes of the countertransference as a concept in Latin American psychoanalysis.

They drew attention to the importance of the analyst's contribution to the analytic process, concentrating on the study and theorisation of the phenomena of unconscious communication between patient and analyst. The countertransference was both the starting- point and the central theme of Racker's work. He saw investigation of the countertransference phenomenon as one of the main factors of change in analytic treatment, as well as a pathway for advances in psychoanalytic theorisation. In the thought of M. and W. Baranger, the theme of the countertransference formed part of a wider conception of the analytic situation, which they saw as a dynamic field.

In following the development of these authors' thought, a process that is still ongoing in the case of the Barangers, we observe how the treatment of the countertransference has varied according to the effect of different theoretical influences. For this reason, examination of this subject affords a view, albeit partial and confined to a specific geographical region, of some of the variations in psychoanalytic conceptions in Argentina and Uruguay from the end of the 1950s until the 1990s.

Heinrich Racker:
transference–countertransference codetermination and the analyst as a participating observer

Heinrich Racker was born in Poland and began his training as a doctor and psychoanalyst in Vienna, completing it in the 1940s in the Argentine Psychoanalytic Association, where he became one of the pioneers of the Argentine psychoanalytic movement.

His idea that the countertransference could be used as an instrument for understanding the psychological processes of the analysand was put forward in his paper "La neurosis de contra-transferencia", presented to the Argentine Psychoanalytic Association in 1948 and subsequently published in the *International Journal of Psychoanalysis* as "A contribution to the problem of counter-transference" (Racker, 1953). Racker began to develop his theory simultaneously with the parallel work of Paula Heimann, although at first the two authors were working completely separately (Etchegoyen, 1986, p. 264).

In Racker's view, the analysts who had studied the counter-transference could be divided into two camps, namely the followers of Freud who worked with classical technique and the analysts steeped in the new ideas of Klein.

Racker drew on both currents. He set himself the task of investigating the implicit dynamics of the countertransference phenomenon, commencing with Freud's idea that aspects of the analyst's infantile neurosis, which acted as resistances, were expressed in the countertransference. He considered that these neurotic aspects of the analyst were the main obstacle to the acceptance and investigation of the countertransference phenomenon.

However, Racker's originality derives principally from his contact with Klein's ideas. In his view, her discoveries of the paranoid–schizoid, depressive and manic positions, the new insights on unconscious fantasy as the expression of the id, ego and superego, the role of the death instinct and the defence mechanisms of projection, introjection and dissociation and the relationship between the internal and external worlds, all modified the analytic technique of interpretation (Racker, 1958a).

Influenced by these ideas on early object relations, Racker posited the existence of an interdependence between, or codetermination of, the phenomena of transference and countertransference, which he saw as constituting a unity, breathing life into each other and creating the interpersonal relationship of the analytic situation (p. 95).

Racker considered that different modes of identification arising between analyst and patient were the source of two forms and functions of the countertransference, as follows.

The concordant countertransference contributed to the task of the analyst as interpreter. It presupposed processes of resonance and equation between what belonged to oneself and to the other. Mechanisms of introjection and projection allowed the analyst to identify concordantly and approximately with the analysand's ego and id in their different facets, experiences, impulses and defences. Concordant identification had its origins in the sublimated positive countertransference and underlay the analyst's empathy and processes of understanding:

> The concordant identification is based on introjection and projection, or, in other terms, on the resonance of the exterior in the interior, on recognition of what belongs to another as one's own ("this part of you is I") and on the equation of what is one's own with what belongs to another ("this part of me is you"). [Racker, 1957, p. 312]

The complementary countertransference, by contrast, was for

him its neurotic aspect, which interfered with the analytic process. The term is used here in its usual sense, involving complementary identifications in which the analyst comes to occupy a position as an object in the analysand's internal world and feels treated as such:

> The complementary identifications are produced by the fact that the patient treats the analyst as an internal (projected) object, and in consequence the analyst feels treated as such; that is, he identifies himself with this object. [p. 312]

For Racker, these infantile objects were, first, the figures of the genital Oedipus complex and its heir, the classical moral superego, and second, those of the early Oedipus complex with its primitive defence mechanisms (1958b, p. 556).

However, the analyst's complementary identification resulted not only from the patient's projections but also from the reactivation of the analyst's infantile neurosis. In these cases, the analysand came to represent objects from the analyst's internal world. The analyst's own impulses towards the figures of his infancy became involved in the contact with patients, preventing a concordant response to them. The rejection of these impulses—in particular, of the analyst's own aggression—was the main disturbing factor:

> It is clear that rejection of a part or tendency in the analyst himself— his aggressiveness, for instance—may lead to a rejection of the patient's aggressiveness (whereby this concordant identification fails) and that such a situation leads to a greater complementary identification with the patient's rejecting object, toward which this aggressive impulse is directed. [1957, p. 312]

Racker describes the feedback mechanism that operates in these phenomena. When the analyst identifies complementarily with the patient, this affects his general psychological state and is involuntarily transmitted through non-verbal elements of the communication, in turn modifying the image of him formed by the analysand:

> the counter-transference affects his manner and his behaviour which in turn influence the image the analysand forms of him. Through the analyst's interpretations, the form he gives them, his voice, through every attitude he adopts towards the patient, the latter perceives (consciously or unconsciously) the psychological

state he happens to be in—not to speak of the debatable question of
telepathic perception. [1953, p. 313]

In this way the countertransference inevitably affects the
analysand, reinforcing his pathological identifications and disturbing
the process of analysis.

The many clinical vignettes Racker used to illustrate his ideas
include a case from the psychoanalytic literature presented by
Wilhelm Reich (1933), who had described a point in the analysis of a
patient suffering from intense inferiority feelings when the tenor of
his interpretations changed. This inhibited patient had serious
sexual difficulties and transferred on to his analyst both his hate for
an elder brother and his defence against his own feminine attitude.
Summing up the case, Reich had concluded that the character
analysis had succeeded in penetrating to the core of the patient's
neurosis: his castration anxiety, his disappointment at his mother's
preferential treatment of his elder brother and his envy of the
brother.

From the case as a whole, Racker reproduces a brief passage
from Reich's account:

> After showing how, for a long period, no interpretation achieved
> any success or any modification of the patient's analytic situation,
> Reich writes: "I then interpreted to him his inferiority feelings
> toward me; at first this was unsuccessful but after I had persistently
> shown him his conduct for several days, he presented some
> communications referring to his tremendous envy not of me but
> of other men, to whom he also felt inferior". And then there
> emerged in me, like a lightning flash, the idea that his repeated
> complaints could mean only this: "The analysis has no effect upon
> me—it is no good, the analyst is inferior and impotent and can
> achieve nothing with me". The complaints were to be understood
> partly as triumph and partly as reproaches to the analyst. [1957,
> p. 327f.]

According to Racker, the lightning flash represented the
analyst's unconscious realisation of his own complementary
countertransference. In his view, it enabled the analyst to integrate
his previously disregarded sensations and feelings. At the same
time he discovered the implicit unconscious identification: "the
analyst is inferior and impotent":

If we inquire into the origin of this "lightning idea" of Reich, the reply must be, theoretically, that it arose from identification with those impulses in the analysand or from identification with one of his internal objects.

The description of the event, however, leaves little room for doubt that the latter, the "complementary countertransference", was the source of Reich's intuition—that this lightning understanding arose from his own feeling of impotence, defeat, and guilt over the failure of treatment. [p. 328]

Racker's comments show how his ideas diverged from those of Reich. First of all, he regards this as a moment of central importance for the progress of the treatment. The analyst's emotional response in the here and now of the session appears as the key to the discovery of the patient's unconscious transference. Here Racker is seen to agree with Heimann's view (1950) that perception of the analyst's affective responses enables him to infer the deep rapport with the analysand.

Another point to which Racker draws attention and which shows the influence of Kleinian theory, is the need for the analyst to be aware of aggressive reactions arising in the countertransference. In his view, complementary identifications become consolidated when used defensively by the analyst to avoid the negative feelings that appear in him in reaction to the patient's aggression.

Repression of the analyst's feelings of frustration—due to his own wounded narcissism—and of his sadism and masochism may cause him to identify unconsciously with sadistic aspects of the analysand's superego, or to submit masochistically to the patient in order to allay his latent aggression and guilt feelings (Racker, 1958a).

Theoretical and technical choices may mask sadistic or masochistic aspects in the analyst. For instance, an active or passive attitude in the analyst's mode of intervention or interpretation may be due to his unconscious identification with projections by the analysand. Racker considers that the analyst's difficulty in owning these negative feelings results from the persistence of unreal infantile ideals resulting from inadequacies in the training analysis (Racker, 1957).

Reich's emphasis on analysis of the infantile neurosis had the aim of modifying the patient's characterological defences. The vignette illustrates the reactivation of the patient's castration anxiety in the present, as well as its reviviscence in the analyst. Racker adds a new element. For him, the complementary identification arises also as the analyst's way of avoiding primitive—persecutory and depressive—anxieties resulting from his own latent aggression. At the clinical juncture described, the analyst is able to save himself from depressive anxieties and guilt feelings due to his sense of annoyance and failure occasioned by the patient's reproaches.

When these or other complementary reactions go unnoticed, they give rise to fixed countertransference positions that strongly affect the ego of the analyst, who feels engulfed in his countertransference. These reactions, which have the effect of counter-resistances, then constitute one of the chief dangers to the progress of the treatment.

If, as in Reich's vignette, the analyst can understand his own countertransference response, he can modify its repetitive character and offer the analysand a possibility of change. There then arises the new or "prospective" aspect of the transference–countertransference situation (Racker, 1957, p. 330f.). The two facets of the countertransference—as an obstacle (complementary identification) and as an instrument (concordant identification)—are thus seen to be closely interdependent. This leads Racker to use the term countertransference in a wide sense, encompassing the totality of the analyst's response to his analysand.

By virtue of the importance attributed to the countertransference, the analyst's difficulties in accepting it and the mutual determination (codetermination) of the transference and countertransference phenomena, Racker came to postulate the need for the analyst to adopt a two-fold position, whereby he could take his own involvement as an object of observation. The analyst had to alternate between being a sensitive passive instrument and a rational critical listener and would then be able to achieve relative objectivity *vis-à-vis* the analysand:

> True objectivity is based upon a form of internal division that enables the analyst to make himself (his own countertransference and subjectivity) the object of his continuous observation and analysis. This position also enables him to be relatively "objective" towards the analysand (p. 309).

Racker died suddenly in 1961 before he was able to develop many of his conceptions, which nevertheless had a profound impact on the thought of his time.

Madeleine and Willy Baranger:
the dynamic field, bipersonal unconscious fantasy and the countertransference

Madeleine and Willy Baranger, thinkers of French origin who settled in Argentina, lived in Montevideo from 1954 to 1965 and contributed to the formation of the Uruguayan psychoanalytic group (Kutter, 1995).

At the beginning of the 1960s they published "La situación analítica como campo dinámico" [The analytic situation as a dynamic field], which summarised the thought of the authors of the time. Its subject was the analytic situation, which they studied in terms of two concepts to which they have remained faithful to this day, namely the dynamic field and bipersonal or basic unconscious fantasy (Baranger & Baranger, 1961–62; M. Baranger, 1993).

The idea of the dynamic field was inspired by Gestalt theory and phenomenology, whereas the conception of unconscious fantasy was a development of notions due to Klein, Isaacs and Bion.

The concept of the dynamic field represented the convergence of various contemporary currents of thought, such as, for example, the ideas of Kurt Lewin, a psychologist of the Berlin School, who used the principles of Gestalt theory for the study of personality and groups. Gestalt theory had refuted associationism, showing that the perception of structures allowed the discovery of a different reality from that resulting from the sum of their parts. Lewin saw individual action, for instance, as a unity or dynamic field in which the individual and the environment interacted.

Enrique Pichon Rivière (1985) was one of the psychoanalysts who introduced these ideas to Argentina. He probably came to Gestalt theory through his study of French thinkers such as Daniel Lagache and Maurice Merleau-Ponty (Vezzetti, 1998). Lagache had attempted to integrate the tradition of behaviourism with phenomenological psychology and clinical psychoanalysis. He saw behaviour as a field phenomenon occurring in different areas—namely, the mind, the body and the world. Merleau-Ponty (1945) incorporated Gestalt theory into his phenomenological approach to behaviour. The Barangers refer to these influences in various contributions (Baranger & Baranger, 1961–62; W. Baranger, 1979; M. Baranger, 1993); they also acknowledge the influence of Pichon Rivière, with whom they had personal contact and who applied the idea of the field to the study of group phenomena in psychiatry and social psychology.

However, M. and W. Baranger must take the credit for using the dynamic field concept to describe the analytic situation. This idea enabled them to approach the analytic situation as a totality that could be studied:

> the need to introduce the concept of field into the description of the analytic situation seems to us to arise out of the structural characteristics of this situation. The analytic situation has its spatial structure, is oriented by specific lines of force and dynamics, and has its own developmental laws, general aim and instantaneous aim. This field is our immediate and specific object of observation. Since the analyst's observation is both observation of the patient and self-observation, in correlation with each other, it cannot but be defined as observation of this field. [Baranger & Baranger, 1961–62, p. 4, translated]

They describe different aspects of the field: its spatial aspect, resulting from the particular features of the physical environment of the consulting room and variations in distance or proximity between analyst and patient; its temporal dimension, as indicated by the rhythm and length of sessions and the separations or interruptions occurring within the analytic process; and its functional configuration, due to the characteristics of the setting—i.e. the different roles assumed by patient and analyst.

However, the main focus of the authors' interest is the study of the unconscious dynamic of the analytic field. They see the analyst's task as the discovery of "the profoundly distinct structure created between another person and ourselves" (p. 19, translated).

Their central hypothesis is that the regressive situation of the analysis gives rise to a new "Gestalt", a bipersonal or basic unconscious fantasy of the couple, different from the fantasies of the patient or analyst considered individually. This fantasy underlies the dynamic of the analytic field—whether it be in motion or in stasis.

These authors derive their hypothesis primarily from their practice of group psychotherapy, which drew on Bion's ideas (1952) concerning basic group assumptions (fight–flight, dependence and pairing). Just as an unconscious group fantasy exists in a group, so a group fantasy arises in the analytic session, although the group in this case has only two members, namely the analytic couple.

The Barangers' idea of bipersonal unconscious fantasy was inspired by the structural conception of unconscious fantasy due to Isaacs and the discovery of the processes of projective identification by Klein (1946, 1948).

Isaacs (1948) had seen unconscious fantasy as an expression of the totality of mental life, comprising both instinctual (libidinal and destructive) impulses and mechanisms of defence against these impulses. In her view, the primitive experience of the body underlay the constitution of fantasies.

M. and W. Baranger develop these ideas. For instance, they describe the analytic field as the stage for the *mise-en-scène* of the patient's primitive fantasies. Experiences relating to space and time may in their view be expressed in different anxieties and fantasies. They point out that changes in the space of the consulting room may trigger phobic or agoraphobic anxieties and that expectations of an unlimited treatment period may conceal, for example, the infantile fantasy that the analyst is the source of inexhaustible gratification.

The assumption that unconscious fantasies are brought into the present in the analytic relationship lies at the root of one of the main characteristics of the analytic field, its radical ambiguity:

> Every event within the analytic field is experienced in the category of "as if" ... it is essential to the analytic procedure that everything and every event in the field is at the same time something else. If this essential ambiguity is lost, the analysis too disappears. [Baranger & Baranger, 1961–62, p. 8f., translated]

However, the Barangers' approach differs to some extent from that of Isaacs and Klein in its emphasis on the idea that the analyst must understand not only the projection of the patient's fantasies but also the processes arising between patient and analyst. The shared unconscious fantasy is conceived as a new structure that can in no way be regarded as determined by the patient's (or, of course, the analyst's) instinctual impulses, although the impulses of both are involved in its structuring. Nor can it be seen as the *sum* of the two internal situations. It is something created *between* the two, within the unity they constitute during the session—something radically different from what each of them is individually. [p. 20, translated]

Central to the process whereby this fantasy is formed will be the mechanism of projective identification and projective counter-identification (Grinberg, 1956).

Grinberg studied the phenomenon of projective counteridenti-fication in the analyst in the context of the treatment of regressive personalities. He saw this phenomenon as a response to the patient's massive projective identifications, but held that the analyst did not contribute directly to its genesis. Projective counter-identification thus was not due to the activation of conflicts on the part of the analyst but constituted a reaction to the patient's projections.

The Barangers, however, use the concept not only as a way of understanding the patient's projections but also to comprehend the forms of unconscious communication established between patient and analyst. Like Racker before them, they draw attention to the mutual character of the phenomena of identification occurring in the analytic session: "The analytic couple depends on the process of projective identification, and the fantasy of the bipersonal field is an interplay of projective and introjective identifications and of counter-identifications" (Baranger & Baranger, 1961–62, p. 23, translated).

Bodily experiences of the patient and the analyst are involved in this interplay. Fantasies of bodily movements arising in the analyst may thus be regarded as responses to current experiences of the patient. This would be an instance of "bodily projective counter-identification": "Each analyst shares the bodily ambiguity and responds with his own body to the analysand's unconscious communication" (p. 12, translated).

The words of the interpretation not only disclose unconscious contents of the patient's psychic reality but are also a form of "doing with the patient". Here the Barangers draw on ideas of Alvarez de Toledo (1954), for whom the words that condense affects and images are seen as intermediate objects between analyst and patient. They are the "bearers of gratifications and aggression and in general of innumerable fantasies" (Baranger & Baranger, 1961–62, p. 43, translated).

The importance assigned to the notion of bipersonal unconscious fantasy led the authors to rethink in relational terms certain concepts not only of the Kleinian school but also of Freud. This reformulation is evident in their discussion of the place of the infantile history, the role of interpretation, the participation of the analyst, and the countertransference.

For M. and W. Baranger, the analyst's interpretation must fundamentally be directed towards the "here and now" of the relationship with the analyst. Aspects of the infantile history are repeated in the fantasied or acted-out link with the analyst. The analyst's attention must be focused on the present of the analytic situation and not on the discovery or reconstruction of facts from the past, or on the regressive reproduction of the fixation points and libidinal stages of infantile development.

To demonstrate their point of view, the authors now contrast their approach with that of Reich (Baranger & Baranger, 1961–62). Reich saw analytic treatment as a regressive process affording access to successive superimposed layers of crystallised impulses and defences responsible for the structuring of the subject's character. This view, based on the Freudian hypothesis of genetic regression, presupposed that the specific analytic regression would succeed in mobilising the deepest strata and resistances of the personality, corresponding to the primitive stages of libidinal development. In this conception, the analyst—like an archaeologist (Freud, 1937)—can use his interpretations to raise or mobilise successive layers of the buried infantile material.

The Barangers contrast Freud's metaphor of the archaeologist with those of the chess game or battlefield (Freud, 1912, 1916–17), which in their view are a better expression of the relational character of the analytic process.

These authors consider that the analyst should focus his attention and interpretive activity on the discovery of infantile reaction patterns as revived in the present relationship with the analyst:

> The patient's use of projective identification enables him to reactivate in the present patterns of reaction originating in

unassimilated situations from his past, crystallised in the form of
stereotyped forms of experience and behaviour. These reaction
patterns partly structure the bipersonal field. The impulses, wishes,
fantasies, anxieties and defences involved in the primal pathogenic
situations recur in the bipersonal field, albeit not in chronological
order or in the same form. Analytic repetition is neither literal nor
stereotyped ... what matters in the dynamic of a treatment is that
emotions, anxieties and wishes should arise within a new, vivid
context ... This dynamic should be seen not in terms of the
reactivation of instinctual impulses but in situational terms.
[Baranger & Baranger, 1961–62, p. 32, translated]

To illustrate their ideas on the significance of the infantile history
and repetition in analysis, the Barangers give a brief commentary on
a clinical case (p. 33f.). The patient concerned had sought treatment
owing to his inability to love and hate, or to feel happy or sad.
Successive traumatic situations from his history were appearing in
orderly fashion in his analysis.

Although the patient managed to experience historical and
transference situations on the emotional level, the analyst had a
countertransference sense of inauthenticity. The most significant
point in this analysis was when an external event precipitated by
the patient himself confronted him with a situation of professional
failure. This episode plunged him into feelings of profound despair
in which his very life appeared to be at risk. Analysis of the fantasies
associated with the experience of failure showed the extent to which
professional success represented a bulwark in which the patient
deposited idealised and omnipotent aspects of himself. The
treatment enabled him to elaborate a number of hitherto split-off
fantasies and integrate different aspects of his history in a new way.
The countertransference sense of inauthenticity disappeared at the
same time.

Brief as it was, this clinical moment is seen by the authors as
demonstrating how repetition processes in analysis are not linear,
how the telling of the patient's history may conceal split-off aspects
that cannot be verbalised and may go unnoticed by the analyst.
These are perceived only through the countertransference experience—in this case, the analyst's sense of inauthenticity.

The concept of the defensive bulwark is also adduced in the
analysis of this clinical vignette. The authors at this time saw the

bulwark as an unconscious refuge of the patient's, which generally concealed powerful fantasies of omnipotence. Its collapse left the patient in a state of extreme helplessness, vulnerability and despair (p. 32).

In this contribution (Baranger & Baranger, 1961–62), the authors also question the idea of the analyst as a "mirror" and emphasise the importance of his participation in the process. The analyst, in their view, cannot be seen as an objective observer who may be equidistant and neutral in relation to the patient's conflicts, but must necessarily be "fully" involved in these conflicts.

In the Barangers' opinion, the analyst's involvement is constant. An example is the importance they attach to capturing the point of urgency in each analytic session, as a basis for the subsequent interrelationship. A clue that should be the prime object of investigation is the manifest or latent reason for anxiety in analyst and patient alike:

> The whole art of the analyst consists in selecting the point of urgency (Pichon Rivière, 1956–58), which can be interpreted within the material supplied by the patient in positive or negative form (verbal or other communication on the one hand, and silence, omission, etc., on the other). His use of and preference for this type of material or that, the way he notes or treats his dreams, the historical material, bodily positions and manifestations, silences, etc., all ultimately come to shape a particular language with the patient. [p. 26, translated]

The importance assigned to the analyst's participation led the Barangers to examine the role of the countertransference as an instrument of technique. The analyst, to the extent that he is the depositary of different aspects and objects of the patient's self, assumes a multiplicity of varying functions. For this reason, he must continuously observe his own countertransference if he is to understand the successive unfolding of the analysand's fantasies.

However, the countertransference phenomenon differs in meaning and intensity from one point in the analytic process to another. In some cases the analyst, exploring his countertransference, may realise that he has identified with split-off aspects of the patient's internal world, so that he becomes able to initiate the process of interpretation. Here the mechanisms of projective identification are limited and the analyst's regression is partial, the observing part of his ego remaining free.

In other situations, by contrast, the analyst responds to the patient's unconscious neurotic conflict with his own. In these cases the analyst plays a direct part in the shaping of the transference neurosis, the processes of mutual identification being more massive. This is the classical conception of the countertransference as resistance:

> The transference neurosis is a repetition of the structure of the patient's neurosis. Similarly, the countertransference microneurosis is the analyst's participation in this structure, involving not only his limited processes of projective identification but also unresolved residues of his infantile conflicts and neurotic structures, manifested as counter-resistances. [p. 37, translated]

In these cases the transference–countertransference neurosis tends to form a repetitive "granite block" that may paralyse the analytic process. However, the analyst's involvement not only proves to be inevitable: part of his function will also be "to allow himself to be involved to some extent with each of his analysands" (p. 37).

The overcoming of feelings of anxiety resulting from the invasion of the patient's projections and the analyst's own neurosis is conditional upon the analyst's ability to access his own observing ego, whereby he can not only practise self-observation but also observe the field as a unity. The interpretive process will seek to mobilise the transference–countertransference microneurosis, clarifying the counter-resistance attitude of the analyst.

The countertransference is thus seen to exhibit gradations due to differences in the intensity of projective identification and of reciprocity phenomena between patient and analyst. The effects of these two situations are observed in the mobility or stasis of the interpretive process and in the changing characteristics of the bipersonal field.

Sometimes interpretation will allow the analyst to save himself from his countertransference experience and throw light on successive points of urgency in the session, with the result that splits in the patient or in the analyst himself are integrated. This gives rise to successive stages of restructuring of the analytic field.

In other cases the analyst feels invaded by the situation, the interpretation has no effect and the field and process are characterised by immobility. The authors subsequently developed these ideas into their concept of the bulwark, seen as a formation of analytic field.

The Barangers' positions gave rise to debate and polemics. Leo Rangell maintained at the 1964 and 1966 Latin American congresses that the analytic process "takes place in the patient". Etchegoyen (1986, p. 500) notes the difference between this position—which is characteristic of the ego-psychologists—and that of the Barangers and the Latin American analysts, who hold that "it takes place between the patient and the analyst".

Re-reading the contributions of W. and M. Baranger forty years after their first publication, we find that the issues raised, although sometimes discussed in schematic or inconclusive form, were innovative in character and foreshadowed present-day thinking. For example, some of the topics that reappear in different theoretical contexts in contemporary thought are: the differences between a unipersonal view that concentrates on the individual intrapsychic realities of patient and analyst, on the one hand and a bipersonal, process-related approach, on the other; the importance assigned to the involvement of the analyst and the countertransference; the reconsideration of neutrality and the significance of the infantile history in analysis; and the importance of the non-verbal aspects of the unconscious communication between patient and analyst.

Although these topics were taken up by thinkers of the authors' own generation, there were discontinuities and interruptions in their development. There are several reasons for these. One is the importance that was assumed by new ideas in the Latin American context, as we shall see below.

Lacan and the questioning of the countertransference concept

During the 1960s a number of analysts—for example, Koolhaas (1971–72) in Montevideo—began to study the thought of Lacan. Contacts with some of his followers ensued at the beginning of the 1970s. Serge Leclaire visited Montevideo and Buenos Aires in 1972 and 1975, offering a conspectus of Lacan's thought and introducing his own developments of it. Maud and Octave Mannoni also came to Montevideo in 1972. These visits marked the beginning of more general exchanges between the Latin Americans and the ideas of Lacan and the French thinkers, which have continued to this day.

Lacan's questioning of the countertransference took place contemporaneously with the distinction he gradually came to make between the imaginary and the symbolic registers, commencing with the hypothesis of the mirror stage.

The mirror stage (Lacan, 1949) corresponds to a point in child development that Lacan places at the age of six months, when the child for the first time sees its own reflected image as a unity and identifies joyfully with it.

In Lacan's view, this stage not only has historical developmental significance but is also important in the structuring processes of the child's psyche. Seeing its reflection in the mirror—for Lacan, also a metaphor of the mother's look—makes for the formation of primary ego identity. However, this first notion of the subject's own integrity has a conflictual aspect. The fact that the child's ego can recognise itself only through the mother's look leaves it in a situation of dependence and bondage. The ego thus arises from the beginning alienated in the image and the desire of the other, for its essence includes the possibility of ignorance of and deception about itself.

To explain the conflictual aspect of the identification process, Lacan (1948) uses not only the metaphor of the mirror but also that of the dialectical master–slave relationship, taken from Hegel. The struggle between master and slave shows how human aggression comes about as a way of escaping from the dependence and alienation entailed by contact with the other. It is a product of the ego's narcissistic struggle for affirmation and recognition *vis-à-vis* an other who is at the same time the guarantor of its existence.

The imaginary register is characterised for Lacan by the predominance of dual, specular and narcissistic links which reproduce these models of relationship with an omnipotent and idealised object that is simultaneously loved and hated.

The Oedipus complex, on the other hand, is seen by Lacan as the paradigm of the symbolic order. Here the father not only confronts the child with sexual differences but also serves as a third party separating the child from the dual relationship with the mother, who then ceases to be the complete figure capable of totally gratifying the child. The father establishes in the child the law that entails acknowledgement of the lack in the other and in oneself. This opens the way to the inexhaustible movement of the unconscious wish, or, in Lacan's terminology, to the discourse of the Other.

The establishment of the symbolic order represents the recognition of limits, absence and lack and entails acceptance by the subject of an essential division. The subject of the unconscious, which is the true subject for Lacan, is in a relationship of radical heterogeneity with the ego, which appears as a locus of alienation and ignorance.

An example of Lacan's distinction between the imaginary and symbolic registers can be found in his analysis of the case of Dick reported by Klein (1961).

Lacan (1954) refers to the point where Klein names the child's various toys in her attempt to unravel his oedipal fantasies. In her interpretations, the boy is the "little train" that enters the "station" (mother) and is contrasted with the "big train" (father). The analyst's interpretations give rise to progress, observed in the subsequent displacement of the child's game on to new objects.

For Lacan, however, the effect of interpretation should not be sought in the imaginary process of transformation of the child's fantasies. The words of the interpretation do not have the fundamental purpose of revealing the contents of fantasies about the inside of the mother's body. In his view, words have a mediating function. In naming the father, the analyst also acts as a third party who sets up a barrier between child and mother.

Here Lacan stresses the importance of language in the constitution of the individual unconscious, an aspect of his theory that has been particularly controversial. Lacan considers that, in naming and distinguishing the elements of the oedipal fantasy configuration, Klein established a new structure in the child, namely the first symbolisations of the oedipal myth.

These developments necessarily led Lacan to reformulate the notions of transference and countertransference. He distinguished between the symbolic and imaginary dimensions of the transference. The symbolic aspect is manifested in the insistence of repetition, whereby the successive signifieds in the subject's history can be revealed. The affective reactions of love and hate between patient and analyst, on the other hand, are seen as imaginary manifestations that operate as resistances.

Lacan used the concept of countertransference in his early works (1951), where it appeared as an obstacle in the analytic process due to the analyst's resistances. However, he gradually came to adopt a critical attitude towards the use of this term, for two reasons.

The first was his refusal to reduce the analysis to a dual, inter-subjective relationship. The analytic relationship tends to reproduce that described by him in the mirror stage, or the dialectical master–slave relationship. The analyst appears as an other who, like the mother or master, possesses omnipotent characteristics and from whom recognition is aggressively demanded. If the work of analysis is focused on transference/countertransference interpretation, this might reinforce the dual links of the analysand, with their connotations of love and hate and the patient's narcissistic illusion of plenitude. Attaching importance to the countertransference might lead to exaggeration of the regressive aspects and affectivity of the analyst as manifested in hate and love, facilitating the induction of feelings in, and the "emotional re-education" of, the patient (Lacan, 1958)—and in particular, encouraging narcissistic identifications between patient and analyst. Lacan rejects the position of authors such as Balint, for whom identification with the analyst is the aim of analysis.

The second reason for Lacan's rejection of the concept of countertransference is that, if the phenomenon of the counter-transference is placed in the foreground, analyst and patient may find themselves in a symmetrical relationship.

The analyst should at all times represent a different structural position from the patient. In the transference, the patient turns the analyst into the depositary of an unlimited "supposed knowledge" about himself and his wishes for narcissistic plenitude. In this sense the analyst is the "subject supposed to know" (Lacan, 1964, p. 209) for the patient. The analyst must avoid responding to these expectations, as well as the suggestion of satisfying, or the wish to satisfy, the patient's demands in any way. He must be able to forgo the exercise of the power vested in him by the patient, placing himself instead in a symbolic transference.

For Lacan, the analyst's neutral attitude plays a central role in the analysis. The exercise of neutrality confirms the analyst in an asymmetrical symbolic position that indicates the limit, or lack (symbolic castration), for himself and the patient. The analyst must not respond to the patient's demands; hence the importance assigned to the analyst's silence as an instrument of technique.

The analyst must closely observe the insistent repetition of certain central signifieds, connected with the subject's primordial experiences. For Lacan, however, repetition is manifested primarily in the insistence of the discourse, or more specifically, of certain auditory sequences (signifiers). The analyst's interpretation will punctuate or draw attention to these moments without seeking to explain them, leaving open the effects of meaning which the analysand constantly attempts to question. Hence the purpose of interpretation is to break with the empty, "capturing" speech of the conscious ego (the *moi* or subject of the *énoncé*, in Lacan's terminology), thus allowing the true subject (the *je* [I] of the *énonciation*, the subject of the unconscious) to emerge. Because he does not offer a finished reality with his interpretation, the analyst places himself in the symbolic dimension of the transference, which is thus contrasted with the imaginary transference, where the vicissitudes of love and hate for the analyst predominate. The imaginary transference operates as a resistance.

Lacan attached great importance to the symbolic aspect of the transference. In it, the analyst occupies the position of the Other, allowing the emergence of his own unconscious wish (desire of the analyst), processes of symbolic identification and, ultimately, restructuring of the patient's subjectivity. If the patient succeeds, during his analysis, in recognising his own limits and those of his infantile figures, he will be able to reappropriate his history in a new form.

For all these reasons, Lacan (1958) was bound to see the term "countertransference" as conceptually inappropriate, in that it facilitates the link with the patient's imaginary transference, encouraging its defensive aspects. In his view, one need only distinguish between the different ways—imaginary or symbolic—in which the analyst and the patient are involved in the transference.

Towards a more discriminating conception of the countertransference

The early work of W. and M. Baranger was undertaken against the background of a dialogue between the ideas of Klein and of Freud.

Their ideas were reformulated from the late 1970s in the context of a new dialectic, this time between some of Lacan's hypotheses and the thought of Klein.

Willy Baranger's "Comentario de los seminarios y conferencias de Serge Leclaire" [Commentary on Serge Leclaire's seminars and lectures], in effect an introduction to Lacan's thought as well as that of Leclaire, was composed in 1976 (W. Baranger, 1976). At that point Baranger observes that the notion of desire of the analyst in Lacan's and Leclaire's thought does not cover what is customarily called countertransference.

Acquaintance with Lacan's ideas did not entail the abandonment of Baranger's original hypotheses. However, from 1979 he adopted a critical attitude towards his own earlier contributions, which also led him to specify the scope of the concept of countertransference more precisely. This reformulation was due mainly to his own clinical observations, but was in addition, in my view, surely a response to the doubts induced by the new ideas, such as the importance attached by Lacan to repetition of the patient's history in the analysis and his stipulation that the analyst must occupy a different structural position from the patient (analytic asymmetry).

W. Baranger (1979) recognised that the field concept of his early work was based on a conception of the transference and counter-transference as overall reactions of the analyst and the patient, which became omnipresent phenomena in the analytic situation. He now admitted that much of the interaction between analyst and patient could be trivial and differed from genuinely transference-related phenomena. He distinguished between interpretations that might be given "within the transference" and interpretations "of the transference", in which the analyst referred explicitly to the transference. At the same time he warned against overemphasis on the present of the session, on the "here and now with me" (p. 28f.). If every interpretation were undiscriminatingly directed towards the present transference relationship, the result might be a failure to explore the patient's history and consequent loss of one of the mainsprings of the analytic process. Here as in Baranger *et al.* (1983), Baranger confirms his agreement with Pichon Rivière, who had seen analysis as a "spiral process" in which past and present were linked dialectically in the session, opening the way to the future:

The fertile moments of interpretation and "insight" punctuate the analytic process, described by Pichon Rivière (1958) as a "spiral process", an image that expresses the temporal dialectics of the process. "Here, now, with me" is often said, to which Pichon Rivière adds "Just as there, before, with others" and "As in the future, elsewhere and in a different way". It is a spiral, each of whose turnings takes up the last turning from a different perspective and which has no absolute beginning or given end. The superimposition of the spiral's curves illustrates this mixture of repetition and non-repetition that may be observed in the characteristic events in a person's fate, this combined movement of deepening into the past and constructing the future that characterises the analytic process (Baranger et al., 1983, p. 9).

Willy Baranger also restricted the concepts of projective identification and counteridentification. In his early work the analytic process had been regarded as "a succession of projective identifications followed by reintrojections that led to a gradual modification of the world of the analysand's internalised objects and psychic agencies" (W. Baranger, 1979, p. 30). Transference and countertransference thus merged with projective identification and counteridentification and even if these phenomena were frequently met with in the analytic situation, "they in no way define its structure or dynamics, still less the work performed therein" (p. 30).

In an apparent response to Lacan's criticism of the tendency to regard analysis as a specular relationship between two "egos", he now called the analytic field the "intersubjective field" and not a bipersonal one:

> We had not recognised the full importance of Lacan's conception of the subject. We have to do not with two bodies or two persons but with two divided subjects whose division is due to an initial triangulation. [p. 30]

Baranger was, however, aware of the difficulties of using concepts from different fields of reference: he wondered whether notions such as that of the divided subject and projective identification were compatible, although he continued to set store by the latter.

He also reflected on the technical implications of Lacan's conception of the unconscious. In his view, the fact that the analyst's interpretation penetrated to and modified the analysand's unconscious conflicts cast doubt on Lacan's hypothesis concerning the heterogeneity of the unconscious. It was difficult to reconcile the specific action of words in interpretation with the conception of an unconscious radically different from the ego. Baranger was here drawing attention to a problematic aspect of Lacan's thought which has resurfaced in present-day psychoanalysis.

In Lacan's conception, the symbolic order is not a continuation of the imaginary order but arises in a relationship of radical otherness with it. Nor is the divided subject, the true subject of the unconscious, a continuation of the ego, which is a place of mirages and ignorance.

Heidegger's idea that the world is structured by language is inherent in Lacan's conception of the unconscious as an Other "ek-centric" to the ego and to intentional subjectivity (Acevedo de Mendilaharsu, 1995). In this respect Lacan's conception of the divided subject and the symbolic order differs clearly from the metapsychologies of Freud and Klein. Whereas Lacan's notion of the divided subject disrupts the dialectic of conscious and unconscious, in Freud and Klein the relationship between the two orders constitutes a dialectically related whole. The Freudian plan, for example, could be seen as a hermeneutic circle with no radical discontinuity between its parts. The manifest appears in relation to the latent, the mechanisms of defence in direct relation to unconscious conflictuality, and so on (Ogden, 1994).

In 1993 M. Baranger turned her attention once again to the scope of interpretation, confirming a dialectical view of interpretation and the analytic process (de León, 1996, 1999). While accepting Lacan's view of the isolated character of unconscious manifestations in the analytic session, she again resorts to classical Freudian and Kleinian notions to indicate that the process of interpretation is not arbitrary but belongs within a prior working context between patient and analyst and that it gives rise to modifications in the patient and in the subsequent history of the analysis.

The second look:
the countertransference and the bulwark

The importance of maintaining analytic asymmetry is emphasised both by W. Baranger (1979) and by Baranger et al. (1983) in their paper presented at the 33rd IPA Congress.

These authors postulate the need for a dual vision by the analyst in the session. His first "look" focuses directly on the patient's associative material. His evenly suspended attention allows him to undertake free-flowing work on the patient's associations, dreams, memories, fantasies, on facts in the patient's history and so on.

When the analyst senses an obstacle to his work, he undertakes a second look at the analytic field as a whole. He then includes himself as an object of observation in the relationship with the patient. The second look entails self-observation by the analyst in his relationship with the patient and leads him to take account directly of the phenomenon of the countertransference.

Certain countertransference indicators alert the analyst and lead him to discover immobilised aspects of the analytic situation:

> Each of us possesses, explicitly or not, a kind of personal counter-transferential dictionary (bodily experiences, movement fantasies, appearance of certain images, etc.) which indicates the moments in which one abandons one's attitude of "suspended attention" and proceeds to the second look, questioning oneself as to what is happening in the analytic situation. [Baranger et al., 1983, p. 2]

Taking up Racker's idea of counter-resistance, these authors show how the link between the patient's resistance and analyst's counter-resistances may become chronic. This gives rise to the formation of a bulwark in the analytic field, maintained by analysand and analyst alike. Different phenomena, described as the "analytic impasse", "unanalysability", "limitations of the analytic process" or the "negative therapeutic reaction", may be attributable to such bulwarks (W. Baranger, 1979, p. 279). The use of the analyst's second look can prevent the formation of these pathological structures of the field or resolve them if they arise.

The bulwark,[1] a central concept in the Barangers' field theory, is: "a neo-formation set up around a shared fantasy assembly which implicates important areas of the personal history of both participants and attributes a stereotyped imaginary role to each" (Baranger et al., 1983, p. 2).

The concept is illustrated by several vignettes:

> An analysand, veteran of a number of analytic treatments. Apparently, each session bears the fruit of some "discovery"; in reality, nothing

is happening. The analyst is delighted by the subtlety of the analysand's descriptions of his internal states, enjoying his own Talmudism. Until he realizes that, while they are toying with their disquisitions, the analysand is monthly placing the analyst's fees at interest, speculating with his delay in paying. The analysis of this bastion reveals a shared fantasy set-up; the analysand's old, surreptitious vengeance on his stingy father and the analyst's guilt-ridden compulsion to set himself up as the cheated father ...

Example of a bastion which has invaded the field. A seriously psychopathic patient. The analyst is terrified, fearing the analysand's physical, homicidal aggression without being able either to suspend or to carry the treatment forward. The nodular fantasy of this bastion is the patient's as torturer in a concentration camp, and the analyst's as tortured, powerless victim. With the conscious formulation of this manoeuvre, the analyst's terror disappears. The two individual histories converge in the creation of this pathological field. [p. 2]

The bulwark (or bastion) entails some loss of analytic asymmetry, in that something that cannot be understood by the analyst is occurring in the analytic field. We observe how mutual projective identifications resulting from the infantile histories of the patient and the analyst contribute to the formation of a shared unconscious fantasy, which assumes stability in the analytic field. In the first case, the analyst's guilty identification whereby he sets himself up as the cheated father combines with the vengeance of the analysand. In the second example, the links between the sadistic and masochistic aspects of the analyst and the patient are expressed in the fantasy of victim and torturer.

The existence of a bulwark is manifested in stereotyped reports and roles and in the analyst's and the patient's experience that nothing is happening. However, it is expressed in indirect effects, such as the aggressive action of delaying payment and exploiting the analyst in the first case, or the feeling of terror in the second. These experiences involve actions, intense affects and fantasies of bodily contact (the references to the money the patient withholds from the analyst in the former case, or the fantasy of bodily damage in the patient's torturer identification in the latter), which cannot at first be understood and verbalised. They escape consciousness and do not appear in verbal exchanges:

> This structure [the bastion] never appears directly in the conscious-
> ness of either participant, showing up only through indirect effects:
> it arises, in unconsciousness and in silence, out of a complicity
> between the two protagonists to protect an attachment which must
> not be uncovered. This leads to a partial crystallization of the field,
> to a neoformation set up around a shared fantasy assembly which
> implicates important areas of the personal history of both
> participants and attributes a stereotyped imaginary role to each.
> Sometimes the bastion remains as a static foreign object while the
> process apparently goes forward. In other situations, it completely
> invades the field and removes all functional capacity from the
> process, transforming the entire field into a pathological field.
> [Baranger et al., 1983, p. 2]

The analyst's second look is essential to the dismantling of this
structure. It enables him to become conscious of his own
involvement in the process, although this does not mean that he
must make countertransference confessions. The ability to convey
the meaning of the implicit fantasy leads to processes of
"desymbiotisation" between analyst and patient. Aspects accom-
modated in the analyst through projective identification can then be
restored to the patient, while feelings can be integrated in both
analyst and patient. The task of interpretation will generate
processes of insight in the patient, and the analyst will in turn
become freer in his "first look" at the analytic field.

The development of the idea of the bulwark enabled these
authors to arrive at a more specific conception of the countertransference. While they continued to use the term liberally, they
sought to distinguish different facets of the phenomenon.

They included in it, first, aspects of the function of the analyst
resulting from his asymmetrical position vis-à-vis the patient: "That
which arises from the structure of the analytic situation itself and
from the placement and function of the analyst within the process"
(p. 4).

When the analyst establishes and maintains the setting and
interprets, he does so in the symbolic register (in Lacan's terms).
However, these authors differ from Lacan in stressing that "the
analyst is committed, flesh, bone and unconscious" (p. 4). The
analyst listens and reacts constantly, but keeps his countertransference in check, allowing it to unfold internally only, in a way that

does not interfere with the exercise of evenly suspended attention and contributes to the process of elaboration of the interpretation.
Second:

> Transferences of the analyst on to the patient which, as long as they do not become stereotyped, are a normal part of the process (e.g. "I know that this patient is not my daughter and that I must guard against my tendency to treat her as if she were"). [p. 4]

The analyst spontaneously transfers feelings or expectations on to the patient, but must beware of his tendency to treat the patient as something of his own. An example might be the possible exaggeration of filial feelings towards the patient.

The authors finally accommodate the following within the countertransference: "Projective identifications of the analyst toward the analysand and his reactions to the projective identifications of the latter. These phenomena provoke pathological structuring of the field, require a second look toward it, also demand priority in interpretive management" (p. 5).

This summarisation of the countertransference, schematic and provisional as it is by the authors' own admission, demonstrates some of their points of agreement and disagreement with Lacan's approach, as well as the prevalence of central concepts of Kleinian thought.

Their closeness to Lacan is illustrated by the importance they attach to analytic asymmetry and to the recognition "that analytic work does not consist in the unflinching exhaustion of 'imaginary petting' (i.e. regressive experiences between two persons without physical contact)" (p. 5).

However, I consider that they differ from Lacan in a number of respects. The conceptions of unconscious fantasy and projective identification remain central to their vision of the analytic process. They likewise retain the term "countertransference", although distinguishing various aspects within it, and continue to attach importance to the understanding of the phenomenon. Although it is seen as an essential instrument, this last contribution emphasises its character as a resistance, whose most accomplished manifestation is the formation of bulwarks in the analytic field.

More fundamental differences emerge in connection with issues such as repetition in analysis, the patient's history, and the function of interpretation.

The bulwark demonstrates the importance of repetitive aspects, which, in contrast to Lacan's view of repetition in analysis, do not appear in verbal exchanges. They arise in silence and involve complicity and unconscious conditioning between patient and analyst. The infantile histories of the patient and the analyst re-emerge in fantasies and affects that are acted out in impenetrable form in the analytic relationship. These phenomena are crucial determinants of the stasis or mobility of the field and the analytic process.

Other differences are observed in regard to the function of the analyst's interpretation. Whereas Lacan drew attention to the disruptive effects of interpretation, via analytic interventions intended to disarm the patient's conscious discourse, Baranger *et al.* see the process of interpretation as a dialectical alternation of the disruptive power of words with their integrating capacity to generate insights in both patient and analyst: "Thus, the mainspring of the analytic process appears to be the production of resistances and bastions and their respective interpretive dissolution, generator of 'insight'" (1983, p. 5).

Obliteration of the concept of countertransference?

The major European schools have influenced the continuity of Latin American psychoanalytic thought in various ways. The assimilation of new ideas has resulted in discontinuities that have sometimes impeded the consolidation of a tradition of thought of our own (Herrmann, 1987).

The treatment of the countertransference in particular is found to have been subject to discontinuities and changes over time. In the particular case of the Uruguayan psychoanalytic movement, the topic is found to have receded somewhat into the background for a period of approximately fifteen years.

In a recent study, de León de Bernardi *et al.* (1998) analysed the occurrence of the variables "transference" and "countertransference" in all the contributions published in the *Revista Uruguaya de Psicoanálisis* between 1960 and 1995.

This descriptor^2-based study showed a decline in the representation of the countertransference between 1975 and 1989. Whereas the proportion of papers on the countertransference amounted to about 10% between 1965 and 1969, it fell to 0%, referred to all published contributions, between 1975 and 1979.

The authors at the same time attempted to correlate the variable "countertransference" with the changing prevalence of the dominant theoretical schools. For this purpose the bibliographies of contributions by Uruguayan authors were examined. A gradual decline in references to Heimann, M. Baranger, W. Baranger and Racker is observed from the beginning of the 1970s. This fall is paralleled by a progressive increase in citations of Freud (24%) and Lacan (8%) and a reduction in references to Klein (2%) (these figures are again referred to the totality of bibliographical citations in published papers by Uruguayan authors). The largest number of bibliographical references to Freud and Lacan are found in the five-year period 1975 to 1979.

Another study (Bernardi et al., 1997) examined changes in the characteristics of interpretations in papers presented at the Uruguayan Psychoanalytic Association between 1960 and 1990. It revealed a significant decline in transference interpretations (i.e. ones in terms of "here and now with me"), in interpretations that took account of the patient's aggression and in those seeking to provide the patient with a better understanding of his feelings about himself. These changes are perhaps partly attributable to the diminution of Kleinian influence.

This research coincided with an analysis by Schkolnik of the characteristics of psychoanalytic work produced in Latin America presented to the first FEPAL (Federation of Psychoanalytic Societies of Latin America) symposium. According to this author, the initial Kleinian theoretical and clinical orientation of the Uruguayan Group began to change "at the end of the 1960s", when "analysts in the Río de la Plata region began to take an interest in the thought of French authors and in particular of the Lacan school, with the visits of S. Leclaire and O. Mannoni" (Schkolnik, 1987, p. 63f.). The reading of French authors encouraged a return to Freud, and more particularly to the Freud of the first topography, relegated to the sidelines in the Kleinian conception. This renewed focus on Freud was partly due to the influence of Lacan and other French thinkers, such as Green and Laplanche, while that of American thought in general diminished. A return to Kleinian thought, "especially as regards child analysis and psychosis" (Schkolnik, 1987, p. 64), occurred at the end of the 1980s. The study of Bion's ideas was a constant at different periods.

It seems to me that Lacan's critique was partly responsible for the relative neglect of the topic of the countertransference, at least in Uruguay, over a number of years. Although Kleinian teachings remained the basis of most analysts' training and the theme of the countertransference was probably implicit in the practice of many, a number of issues raised during the 1960s and 1970s were then left aside. These concerned both the various forms of participation of the analyst and the investigation of the forms of conscious and unconscious communication established in the analytic process.

In my view, the importance attached to the analyst's symbolic position and his neutrality, coupled with the reduced regard for his imaginary participation (an aspect particularly evident in Lacan's early work), made for idealisation processes in the analyst at the expense of a more realistic vision of his involvement. On the other hand, because this theory is ambiguous and difficult to translate into clinical practice, it has the effect of diverting psychoanalytic reflection away from description of the concrete experience of analysis.

However, the introduction of a new perspective had the advantage of drawing attention to, and allowing the rethinking of, the sometimes dogmatic use of Kleinian notions. This concerned, for example, the interpretation of aggression, or exaggeration of the phenomena of transference and countertransference, which on occasion impeded the analyst's listening to the patient and the process of free association. However, criticism of the sometimes indiscriminate use of the concept of the countertransference has also been expressed from different theoretical standpoints and may be a hallmark of greater maturity in the psychoanalytic movement. For instance, Etchegoyen (1993) points out that the analyst's use of his countertransference and its manifestations in his interpretations must be subordinated to the patient's associative material. He is thus warning of the risks of exaggerating the countertransference phenomenon and pointing out that the analyst is liable to attribute aspects of himself to the patient, with resulting loss of the specific aim of the analytic method, namely, transformation of the patient's psychic reality.

A wider debate on the theme of the countertransference was initiated in the pluralistic context of the twenty-first FEPAL Congress held in Monterrey, Mexico, in 1996, on "The transference–countertransference field". Old traditions were here re-examined in the light of recent theoretical contributions. Whereas the influence of Kleinian thought predominated when many of the region's psychoanalytic groups were first formed, we now observed not only Kleinian and post-Kleinian allegiances but also the espousal of Freudian ideas, those of Lacan and other French workers and in some regions also notions originating from the United States. With a few exceptions, however, no one seemed to be attempting to put all these elements together and to undertake an in-depth investigation of the theoretical and technical differences between the various approaches.

Conclusions

To sum up, the authors discussed above use the concept of countertransference in a wide sense, to denote the analyst's overall response to the patient, as postulated by Heimann. However, within this response they have sought to distinguish a range of phenomena extending from the specific processes of analytic listening to the resistance-related reactions of the analyst.

The concept of countertransference emerges as an element in a conception of the analytic situation that emphasises the mutual constitution of field phenomena. It is closely bound up with the notion of projective identification and unconscious fantasy. Racker's idea of transference–countertransference codetermination is expanded into the conception of a shared Gestalt and attains its highest level of discrimination in the Barangers' concept of the bulwark. This idea was taken up from a different angle by Bleger (1967) in his study of symbiosis in the analytic field.

The idea of the complementarity of field phenomena was to reappear in the work of Liberman (1970) on the analytic dialogue and complementarity in the styles of analyst–patient communication. This author laid particular stress on the study of forms of verbalisation in the session, which he saw as a narrative organised in time sequences (1976). He also advocated the use of methods of empirical research to study the characteristics of the analytic dialogue, an approach he continued to commend to the end of his career (1978).

The authors who regarded the transference and countertransference as reciprocal phenomena did not on that account abandon the notion of analytic asymmetry or the principle of the analyst's neutrality. On the contrary, they sought to identify the difficulties arising on the part of the analyst and the defensive links that may become established with the patient. Hence the importance of the idea of the analyst as a participating observer, which appears as a countervailing tendency to the notion of the countertransference in the work of the various authors.

Combinations of different theoretical frameworks are evident in the thought of Racker on the one hand and of M. and W. Baranger on the other. Whereas a Freud–Klein dialogue appears as the background to the former, a comparison of Kleinian and Lacanian ideas is introduced as an additional element in the work of the latter. Our examination indicates how changes in the conception of the countertransference modify the analyst's position in relation to the clinical facts.

These modifications sometimes appear to include prior contributions that are not made explicit. This is the case, for example, with work on aggression in patient and analyst. Whereas this is a central aspect of Racker's thought, it features much less prominently in the Barangers' studies. Nevertheless, its importance seems to be taken for granted in the constitution of the bulwark, as the various clinical examples indicate.

The work of M. and W. Baranger shows how the incorporation of new ideas leads to a rethinking of clinical experience. However, the differences between the various approaches persist and are particularly conspicuous where the countertransference is concerned. The countertransference conception inherent in the idea of the bulwark is not readily reconcilable with Lacan's notions of the analyst's symbolic and imaginary transference. His ideas not only belong to different frames of reference, but also include hypotheses on different levels of abstraction (Liberman, 1970). Lacan's conceptions are based on a metapsychological hypothesis with a high degree of abstraction, whereas the concept of the bulwark seeks to describe the variations in the unconscious modes of communication between patient and analyst during the analytic process; in this sense it is much closer to the description of clinical experience. The same is found to apply to Racker's notions of the concordant and complementary countertransference.

In my view, however, the most significant difference between the two positions is that Lacan takes further Freud's idea of the countertransference as a blind spot in the analyst. In Lacan's vision, the countertransference arises when the analyst takes the wrong path, which acts as a deceptive screen in the contact with the patient. Conversely, both Racker and the Barangers hold that the countertransference, although problematic, proves to be a valuable instrument in communication with the patient, leading to an understanding of central aspects of his unconscious conflict. All the same, a systematic comparative study of the various technical implications of the two approaches has yet to be conducted.

Acknowledgement

I am grateful to Cláudio Laks Eizirik, Bob Michels and David Tuckett for their comments on an earlier draft of this paper.

Notes

1. Translator's note: The Spanish word *baluarte*, elsewhere rendered as "bulwark", is translated as "bastion" in the following.
2. A descriptor is a complex indicator with characteristics set conventionally by a group independent of the study. Its members deemed a descriptor to be present in a contribution when a given concept—in this case the countertransference—received a comprehensive treatment or new ideas were presented on it.

References

Acevedo de Mendilaharsu, S. (1995). Subjetividad y tiempo en el espacio analítico. In: *Lo Arcaico, Temporalidad e Historización* (pp. 61–70) (IX Jornadas Psicoanalíticas de APU). Uruguay: Comisión de Publicaciones de la Asociación Psicoanalítica del Uruguay.

Alvarez de Toledo, L. (1996). The analysis of "associating", "interpreting" and "words". *Int. J. Psychoanal.*, 77: 291–318, 1954.

Baranger, M. (1993). The mind of the analyst: from listening to interpretation. *Int. J. Psychoanal.*, 74: 15–24.

Baranger, M. & Baranger, W. (1961–62). La situación analítica como campo dinámico. *Rev. Uruguaya Psicoanál.*, 4: 3–54.

Baranger, W. (1976). Comentario de los seminarios y conferencias de Serge Leclaire. *Rev. Argentina Psicoanál.*, 33: 749–765.

Baranger, W. (1979). 'Proceso en espiral' y 'campo dinámico'. *Rev. Uruguaya Psicoanál.*, 59: 17–32.

Baranger, W,. et al. (1983). Process and non-process in analytic work. *Int. J. Psychoanal.*, 64: 1–15.

Bernardi, R. et al. (1997). Cambios de la interpretación en el psicoanálisis del Uruguay entre 1960 y 1990. *Rev. Uruguaya Psicoanál.*, 84/85: 89–102.

Bion, W. R. (1952). Group dynamics: a re-view. *Int. J. Psychoanal.*, 33: 235–247.

Bleger, J. (1967). *Simbiosis y Ambigüedad*. Buenos Aires: Paidós.

De León, B. (1996). Problemas del campo de la transferencia–contra-transferencia: perspectiva actual y vigencia de nuestras raíces (official report to the XXI FEPAL Congress). *Rev. Uruguaya Psicoanál.*, 84/85: 179–199.

De León, B. (1999). Un modo de pensar la clínica: vigencia y perspectivas del enfoque de W. y M. Baranger. In: *Volviendo a Pensar con Willy y Madeleine Baranger*. Buenos Aires: Ed. Nuevos desarrollos.

De León de Bernardi, B. et al. (1998). Cambios en la frecuencia del uso de la noción de contratransferencia, y su relación con los cambios en las teorías dominantes (paper presented to the 4th Meeting of the South American Chapter of the Society for Psychotherapy Research [SPR]: "Investigación empírica en psicoterapia", Montevideo, 25–27 September 1998).

Etchegoyen, R. H. (1986). *The Fundamentals of Psychoanalytic Technique*, P. Pitchon (Trans.). London: Karnac, 1991.

Etchegoyen, R. H. (1993). Psychoanalysis today and tomorrow. *Int. J. Psychoanal.*, 74: 1109–1115.

Freud, S. (1912). Papers on technique. *S.E.*, 12.

Freud, S. (1916–17). *Introductory Lectures on Psycho-Analysis* (Lecture 28: Analytic therapy). *S.E.*, 16.

Freud, S. (1937). Constructions in analysis. *S.E.*, 23.

Grinberg, L. (1956). Sobre algunos problemas de técnica psicoanalítica determinados por la identificación y contraidentificación proyectivas. *Rev. Psicoanál.*, *13*: 507–511.

Heimann, P. (1950). On counter-transference. *Int. J. Psychoanal.*, *31*: 81–84.

Herrmann, F. (1987). Características de la producción psicoanalítica latinoamericana. In: *Correio da Fepal* (pp. 7–9). São Paulo: MBV Comunicacoes.

Isaacs, S. (1948). The nature and function of phantasy. *Int. J. Psychoanal.*, *29*: 73–97.

Klein, M. (1946). Notes on some schizoid mechanisms. In: *Envy and Gratitude and Other Works* (pp. 1–24). London: Hogarth, 1975.

Klein, M. (1948). On the theory of anxiety and guilt. In: *Developments in Psychoanalysis* (pp. 271–291). London: Hogarth.

Klein, M. (1961). *Narrative of a Child Analysis*. London: Hogarth.

Koolhaas, G. (1971–72). ¿Quién es el Otro? *Rev. Uruguaya Psicoanál.*, *4*: 349–384.

Kutter, P. (Ed.) (1995). *Psychoanalysis International. A Guide to Psychoanalysis Throughout the World, Volume 2: America, Asia, Australia, Further European Countries*. Stuttgart: Frommann-Holzboog.

Lacan, J. (1948). L'agressivité en psychanalyse. In: *Écrits* (pp. 65–87). Paris: Seuil, 1966.

Lacan, J. (1949). Le stade du miroir comme formateur de la fonction du Je telle qu'elle nous est révélée dans l'expérience psychanalytique. In: *Écrits* (pp. 93–100). Paris: Seuil, 1966.

Lacan, J. (1951). Intervention sur le transfert. In: *Écrits* (pp. 215–226). Paris: Seuil, 1966.

Lacan, J. (1954). *Le Séminaire, Livre I: Les Écrits Techniques de Freud*. Paris: Seuil, 1975.

Lacan, J. (1958). La direction de la cure et les principes de son pouvoir. In: *Écrits* (pp. 585–645). Paris: Seuil, 1966.

Lacan, J. (1964). *Le Séminaire. Livre XI: Les Quatre Concepts Fondamentaux de la Psychanalyse*. Paris: Seuil, 1973.

Liberman, D. (1970). *Lingüística, Interacción Comunicativa y Proceso Psicoanalítico*. Buenos Aires: Galerna, 1971.

Liberman, D. (1976). *Lenguaje y Técnica Psicoanalítica*. Buenos Aires: Kargieman.

Liberman, D. (1978). El diálogo psicoanalítico y la complementariedad estilística entre analizando y analista. *Rev. Uruguaya Psicoanál.*, *58*: 37–48.

Merleau-Ponty, M. (1945). *La Phénoménologie de la Perception*. Paris: NRF/Gallimard.

Ogden, T. (1994). *Subjects of Analysis*. Northvale, NJ: Aronson.

Pichon Rivière, E. (1958). Referential schema and dialectical process in spiral as basis to a problem of the past (abstract). *Int. J. Psychoanal.*, 39: 294.

Pichon Rivière, E. (1985). *El proceso grupal. Del psicoanálisis a la psicología social, Volume 1*. Buenos Aires: Nueva Visión, 1988.

Racker, H. (1953). A contribution to the problem of counter-transference. *Int. J. Psychoanal.*, 34: 313–324.

Racker, H. (1957). The meanings and uses of countertransference. *Psychoanal. Q.*, 26: 303–357.

Racker, H. (1958a). Classical and present techniques in psycho-analysis. In: *Transference and Countertransference*. London: Hogarth, 1968.

Racker, H. (1958b). Psychoanalytic technique and the analyst's unconscious masochism. *Psychoanal. Q.*, 27: 555–562.

Reich, W. (1933). *Character Analysis*. New York: Orgone Institute Press, 1945.

Schkolnik, F. (1987). Características de la producción psicoanalítica latinoamericana. *Correio da Fepal* (pp. 63–69). São Paulo: MBV Comunicoes.

Vezzetti, H. (1998). *Enrique Pichon Rivière: el psicoanálisis y la psicología social* [paper presented to the I Colóquio de História da Psicanálise do Programa de Estudos Pós-Graduados em Psicología Clínica da PUC/SP. São Paulo, Brazil, 22–24 October 1998].

4: The countertransference scene in France

FRANÇOIS DUPARC, Annecy

I make no claim in this paper to review every single contribution made by French psycho-analysis to the subject of the counter-transference. I shall confine myself to a personal viewpoint, which will itself no doubt have a countertransference aspect, in the broad sense of a countertransference connected with my clinical experience as a whole.

The theories I shall present are mainly those which have influenced the thinking and practice not only of myself but also of many colleagues of my generation—the writings and accounts that have helped me to negotiate the inevitable risks of the counter-transference. I should therefore add that I have deliberately chosen to concentrate, among the authors who have influenced me, on those who have explicitly focused a part of their work on the countertransference.

The French scene before 1970

In reviewing the French contributions and comparing them with those from the English-speaking countries and South America, I quickly noticed that publications devoted explicitly to the counter-transference began to appear in any number only quite late on in France: they date back to the beginning of the nineteen seventies, with the work of Serge Viderman and Michel Neyraut. Admittedly, analysts such as Sacha Nacht, Jacques Lacan, Daniel Lagache and Michel Bouvet had touched upon the subject before them, but only marginally and in ultimately very restrictive terms.

Why this delay? The reason became clear as soon as I recalled the part played by Jacques Lacan in French psychoanalysis, especially as I myself attended his seminars for a few years until 1976, when I parted company with his school.

Going back in time somewhat, we may briefly note that in the post-war period, from 1945 until at least 1953, the year when Lacan left the Paris Psychoanalytical Society and the IPA, his teaching was one of the most influential currents in that society, even if his practice was already controversial. He came to be seen as a guru, whose ideas became highly fashionable and were increasingly widely espoused. For this reason, when he decided to disparage the use of the word *countertransference*, which was greatly in vogue in the English-speaking countries in the nineteen fifties and sixties, this became an impediment for all the authors he influenced, both near and far.

This hypothesis had already begun to take shape in my mind when I read the paper by our Uruguayan colleague Beatriz de León de Bernardi (2000), published in Volume 81, Part 2, of the *International Journal of Psychoanalysis*, on the development of the concept of the countertransference in Latin America. My impression was thereby confirmed, as she here blames the influence of Lacan in nineteen seventies Latin America for the manifest decline in publica-tions on the subject and for the questioning of the relevant theories by such prominent authors as Madeleine and Willy Baranger.

What did Lacan actually say? The subject of the counter-transference was not to his liking. He still happens to mention it in one of the earliest of the texts brought together in his *Écrits* (Lacan, 1951), where he holds it responsible for Freud's mistakes with Dora, deeming it to be a prejudice, an embarrassment or an instance of confusion on the analyst's part due to shortcomings in his training. Later, however, he refers to it only ironically, using the English word to indicate that to him it is an invention foreign to the original language of psychoanalysis: "The analyst pays with his person, in that he is literally dispossessed of it; whatever his panic recourse to 'The Countertransference',[1] he must inevitably go that way" (Lacan, 1960, p. 337, translated).

There are several reasons for his rejection. First, he sees the term as too symmetrical with the transference, suggesting an imaginary, mirror-type link between patient and analyst. Now the distinction between the imaginary, the symbolic and the real soon came to assume paramount importance for Lacan, who saw the imaginary, the mirror stage and the affects of love and hate arising in it as the prototype of ego alienation. The term countertransference thus seemed to him to encourage a dual relationship instead of a language-mediated and hence triangular one.

The second reason is the priority accorded by the authors who developed the concept (Paula Heimann and the British Kleinian school) to pre-verbal communication, affect and the maternal dominance of this countertransference. Lacan always defended the role of the father as the support of desire, and the Name-of-the-Father, the guarantor of the symbolic order, as a means whereby the subject could escape from the dominion of the mother. As we know, he also assigned language an essential part in psychoanalysis, even asserting that the unconscious was structured like a language (1953, 1977). In his later writings he would seek to limit the analyst's function to a purely symbolic one; the main purpose of the analyst's neutrality was to thwart the patient's imaginary transference (which was made up of affects), while his or her interventions ought merely to draw attention to the symbolic transference, in the form of insistence on the subject's historical signifiers. Lacan was also to state that, if the analyst was the object of transference because he was "supposed to know", his knowledge actually consisted in nothing but the capacity to accept his lack, his frustration and his "being-for-death" (1960). This was the purely symbolic role to which the "analyst's desire" should be limited—a role Lacan attempted in his final works to fix in a *matheme*.[2]

However, his irony was by no means reserved for the psycho-analysis of the English-speaking countries—in particular, the idea of the autonomous ego, or of the analyst as an identificatory model for the patient. One of his main targets was in France, within the Paris Psychoanalytical Society as constituted after the 1953 split, in the person of Sacha Nacht. Now Nacht was admittedly not as brilliant a theoretician as Lacan, but he was, to his credit, interested in the countertransference (Nacht, 1962). He was presumably the instigator of the Congress of French-Language Psychoanalysts on the countertransference held in 1962, just before the split, which had two Spanish rapporteurs from Barcelona, Bofill and Folch Mateu.

Sacha Nacht's conception, as it emerges from his 1962 paper for this congress or from "*La présence du psychanalyste*" (1963), was plainly something of a caricature. For him, silence was not a frustration but a manifestation of the psychoanalyst's presence, of his participation in a non-verbal relationship and a state of pre-object fusion that reproduced the situation of the first months of life. He saw analysis as a field of intersubjective experience *à deux*, in which the psychoanalyst's deep inner attitude and involvement in the process of working through played an important part in the development of the patient's autonomous ego. The transference was to be overcome by encouraging the patient to turn aside from the imaginary relationship with the analyst and cathect external reality.

Here, evidently, are all the pitfalls to which Lacan—in part rightly—drew attention. However, this was not a time for subtle distinctions, nor was the diametrically opposite position a good guide for analysts on how to handle their countertransference. Lacan's stance was ultimately no more than a caricature of Freud's recommendation to master the countertransference.

Yet Lacan's role in the matter of the countertransference was perhaps not entirely negative, for he contributed, albeit indirectly, to the subsequent originality of the eventual French positions. His insistence on remaining faithful to Freud, his distrust of the fascination exerted by the archaic and the pre-verbal, and his reminder of the necessity of triangulation even at the earliest stages of life—all these factors influenced the least Lacanian of French analysts, encouraging them to retain the whole of the oedipal structure and its component primal fantasies even in children or in near-psychotic or near-psychosomatic contexts.

However, Lacan's theory of the countertransference cannot be simply accepted as it is; if it is to be turned to practical account, it must undergo painstaking translation, for it is essential to realise the extent of its ideological content, which had the aim of ensconcing the psychoanalyst in the armchair of the big Other, the master of the signifier, and of totally disregarding the necessary questioning of certain points, at least where he himself was concerned.

This attitude no doubt had to do with the brevity of Lacan's own analysis and his difficulty, for which there is substantial evidence, in tolerating more than a modicum of transference from his patients—a trait, incidentally, that he shared with Sacha Nacht. The fact is that his excessive manipulations of the setting in the service of the "significant scansion"—he would break off a session just when a fundamental signifier appeared to him as such—simply concealed any analysis of the countertransference in both himself and those of his pupils who did not succeed in keeping their distance from him.

Moreover, Lacan's idiosyncratic practice and the liberties he took with session length and the classical setting, by sparking a fierce debate within French psychoanalysis, usefully drew attention to the link between the countertransference and the treatment setting—an interesting trend in the French literature on the countertransference. This, however, in effect called for a prior period of mourning—on the part of Lacan's pupils and enemies alike—for the positive or negative idealisation aroused by his thought.

Before describing in more detail the various contributions of recent authors, I should like now to attempt a more precise definition of the particularity of French publications on the countertransference, and of the specific approach discernible in at least the majority of them.

For this purpose I shall draw upon a comprehensive paper by Louise de Urtubey presented in Lisbon in 1994 at another Congress of French-Language Psychoanalysts. This congress was devoted to "The work of the countertransference" and it sought to classify the different theories of the countertransference from the earliest days of the concept. Apart from the countertransference of seduction observed by Freud, to combat which he gradually developed the rules of abstinence and frustration, this author considered that four main types of theory could be described.

The first group comprises the classical theory, in which the countertransference is viewed with suspicion, and is deemed an unanalysed residue in the analyst, to be controlled or minimised by a rigid setting of neutrality and silence intended to limit the expression of affects on the part of the analyst. Urtubey classifies authors such as Glover, Nunberg, Ida Macalpine, Annie Reich,

Robert Fliess, Greenson, Schafer and Sandler in this group. I personally am inclined to add the name of Lacan to her list, for he has more than one characteristic in common with those mentioned. However, his position is atypical in that, unlike most of these authors, he sets no particular store by the working alliance and the real relationship.

The second type comprises the "totalist" theory, in which the countertransference is seen as the totality of the emotions and feelings aroused in the analyst by the patient, which enable the analyst to understand the patient. In this conception, unconscious-to-unconscious communication makes the analyst a kind of passive receptacle for the patient's experiences; although the analyst emerges from his or her passivity by interpreting, he or she does so as if everything came from the patient. In the author's view, the specificity of this type lies in its sometimes excessive emphasis on both affects and the maternal countertransference model, as opposed to the paternal model espoused by the first group— including Freud. This trend dates back to Ferenczi, and most of its protagonists are British; they include Strachey, the Balints, Winnicott (who, however, is rather atypical of the group), Bion, Searles and, in particular, Grinberg, who was an extreme exponent of this position. In France, the relevant authors might include Sacha Nacht and—albeit with more subtle theories—Joyce McDougall and Janine Chasseguet-Smirgel, especially as regards the maternal–feminine countertransference model.

The third type is the theory of the neurotic but useful countertransference, a corrective to the excesses of the first two positions. It emphasises the analyst's self-analysis as an essential factor in the analytic process. When working with seriously disturbed patients, the analyst splits off and treats his or her own sick part, which must also be capable of accepting the help of a third party—such as the patient. From this point of view, the analyst is evidently seen by such theories as able to identify in the counter-transference with the dependent child. According to Louise de Urtubey, authors such as Margaret Little or, perhaps, Harold Searles may be assigned to this group. A similar trend may, in my opinion, be observed in France in an author such as Pontalis.

However, a fourth group of theories is the one preferred by Urtubey, as well as, in her view, by most French authors and many of those in South America (her own continent of origin). These are the theories of the countertransference as a component of the analytic space. Here the countertransference is not seen as troublesome, or total, or as something to be subjected primarily to self-analysis, but serves for understanding the analytic situation. Transference and countertransference are the elements that make up a unity, a process of work undertaken jointly. In this dynamic couple, the roles of analyst and patient are nevertheless asymmetrical, as regression is the prerogative more of the analysand than of the analyst, who must remain the guardian of the setting. This theory of the analytic space or field, perhaps inspired by Lagache's borrowings from behaviourism in the nineteen fifties, was developed by M. and W. Baranger in Argentina in 1962 (although it was much later before their work became known in Europe), and then independently by Serge Viderman in France around 1967. Urtubey considers that most modern French authors—in particular, Neyraut, Donnet, de M'Uzan, Guillaumin, Faimberg and herself—belong to this group.

However, valuable as this classification is for initial orientation, it does not suffice for a precise definition of the specific approaches of the French authors on the countertransference.

While the concept of the analytic space is indeed a central organising aspect of the position of most French authors, this is not only because of the coupling of the transference and the countertransference. Another reason is that the analytic space as a whole very soon came to be apprehended as a scene, as a psychic and as it were metapsychological space in which the topography of the interaction and the setting is more important than the mere experience of one or other of the partners in the treatment. As Freud put it in one of his last notes, "Psyche is extended; knows nothing about it" (1941, p. 300). Again, this topographical space has always been conceived of as the representation of a temporal field, since the unconscious, being timeless, represents time by spatial relations. Hence the subject's history, too, is divided between the setting and the transference/countertransference process, and never dissolves in the present of experience.

What is the origin of this conception? It presumably results from a compromise between extreme, antithetical tendencies, resolving the conflict between Nacht, who wrote of patient–analyst fusion, and Lacan, who wanted to maximise the distance between the two so that the pure symbol, or indeed the matheme, might come into being in this expanded space. After all, the psychoanalyst Michel Bouvet, who wrote on technique and variations of the setting, had begun work on the distance between subject and object as long ago as in 1958.

Ultimately, as we shall see, it was Serge Viderman who opened the debate on the issue of the countertransference, the analytic space and the analyst's part in the constructions of the treatment. Why Viderman? Apart from his personal qualities, it was perhaps because he brought to a head a simmering controversy on the contemporary psychoanalytic scene—with Lacan on stage and Winnicott in the wings. A debate ensued about the scene itself and its limits, for the split had—like the transference according to Freud—set the analytic scene ablaze, in relation to the countertransference of the entire analytic institution.

A decisive part in this all-French debate was in fact played by certain outsiders, who contributed greatly to the dawning awareness of the importance of the psychoanalytic setting—as, in effect, a third party in the treatment. The principal figure here was Winnicott, who influenced the third generation of French analysts (Green [1977], Laplanche and Pontalis) as greatly as did Lacan, from whose hegemony he helped them to break free, and who is one of the French analytic community's favourite psychoanalysts—far more so, indeed, than Bion.

One of Winnicott's contributions was to help make analysts aware that the setting—as an ambiguous space that was neither inside nor outside but transitional—was also a joint creation that did not belong completely to either patient or analyst but marked the boundaries of an area in which conflicts that would otherwise be unrepresentable could come to be symbolised through the interplay of transference and countertransference alone.

The paper by the Argentinean analyst José Bleger on the psychoanalytic setting (1967) was another essential catalyst of the (more specifically French) distinction between the fixed (theoretico–technical) setting and the handling of the transference—i.e. between the setting and holding—and in relation to their mutual influence. Mention should also be made of the American analyst Bertram Lewin, whose theory of the dream screen was taken up by Green in his study of the limits and the negative of representation in the analytic setting, an aspect barely touched upon by Winnicott.

Finally, French psychoanalysis was to approach the counter-transference not only in terms of the dual, here-and-now line of the transference and the countertransference, but as an entity within a wider, triangular topographical and temporal space, on a psycho-analytic stage bounded by an envelope—a setting—with which it entertained relations of exchange and conflict. Countertransference issues arose in three contexts: (1) constructions of the subject's history and the analyst's part in their creation; (2) the transference–countertransference experience between affect and language, body and verbalisation, conscious and unconscious; (3) the setting in all its aspects—imaginary, concrete and theoretical (including the analyst's theory)—the analyst's responsibility for its management, and the patient's responsibility for putting it to the test.

As we shall see below, the questions arising in the last few years (in particular, among the analysts of the Lyons region, who include Guillaumin, Roussillon and myself) focus on the widening of the setting—to embrace extra-analytic spaces or therapeutic ideologies moulded by the social field in which psycho-analysis is practised. The opening up of the transference–countertransference field also entails the need to contemplate a wide variety of possible counter-transference types, and hence to aim for combination rather than exclusion of different theories, so as to avoid immobilising the analytic field within a single model.

The players from 1970 to the present day

1) Serge Viderman

Serge Viderman was the instigator of a minor revolution in French psychoanalysis in the nineteen seventies, in the form of his conception of the analytic space. Within this space (which closely resembled the field of M. and W. Baranger), the constitution of an original transference–countertransference couple, together with the analyst's interpretations, made it possible to construct stories that could otherwise never have come into being—stories that were more mythical than historical. Nothing could have been more different from Freud's scientific ideal of the archaeological reconstruction and reconstitution of the patient's infantile past.

The foundations of his ideas were in fact laid as early as in 1967, in his contribution to a colloquium on acting out, on "The genesis of the transference and the structure of the psychoanalytic field" (Viderman, 1968). Here he wrote that, however much the analyst sought to disappear and to provide an ideal setting in which the patient could regress and thereby bring back the repressed or forgotten past in the transference, the analyst in fact drew attention to his or her presence by the essential act of interpretation. The analyst was not a mirror, or, if so, it was a talking mirror, which on that account modified the transference: the countertransference was the acting out of the analyst. The desire for purity, for non-seduction by the analyst, was a myth, like the fantasy of Kant's dove, which thought it would be able to fly better without the resistance of the air. The transference neurosis was thus an original creation and not the mere repetition of the repressed past.

Viderman pursued these ideas further in his 1970 book, *La construction de l'espace analytique*, in which he stated that, notwithstanding the vital importance of language and the reconstruction of the subject's history in the treatment, part of the repressed—the primal repressed—could never return to consciousness except by way of the analyst's construction; at this point history gave way to myth, to fantasy versions: "The primal repressed can never return to consciousness except through 'constructions' of the analyst, to which, since they are merely probable, a considerable measure of uncertainty necessarily attaches" (Viderman, 1970, p. 17, translated).

At any rate, the interpretation and analysis of resistances are steeped in countertransference—for, however cautious the analyst, there is no resistance without insistence, given that it is the analyst's unconscious that hears the other unconscious. At most, an asymmetry can be said to exist, since the treatment is so designed as to give the transference the freedom to take shape as it will, whereas the countertransference is limited in its expression. Yet remaining silent or trying to stand aloof from one's countertransference is also a form of countertransference, albeit negative. Moreover, it is not easy to delimit the field of the countertransference—that is, to distinguish between the universal tendency to form a transference and the neurotic residue left untouched by the analyst's analysis. The countertransference is inevitably, to some extent, a blind spot: "It is because of the countertransference that things escape us; but it is by virtue of the countertransference that we perceive everything else" (p. 49, translated).

In response to the various—in some cases quite critical—reactions to his book, Viderman felt it necessary to explain his ideas in more detail. This he did in 1974 in "La bouteille à la mer", in which he attempted to show that, following his resistance to the transference, Freud had never overcome his distrust of the countertransference, which he sought to master mainly by counter-measures such as analysis of the analyst or ensuring the purity of the setting. However, the strengthening of this attitude solved nothing, for excessive distrust locked the analyst into a rigid, defensive attitude. Nor was it legitimate to share Lacan's faith in the omnipotence of words without accepting their power of construction, which was not innocent: "The analytic process is possible only in a space of intersecting affects and counter-affects ... The analytic space is an imaginary, ambiguous space, just like the transference–countertransference link" (Viderman, 1974, p. 369, translated).

The analyst's power was ultimately one exerted only over the setting—i.e. a technical power. By these formulations, Viderman is seen to be offering an interesting alternative to Lacan's views, by drawing attention to the ambiguous power of the setting and leaving open the possibility of its elaboration.

In his last book, *Le céleste et le sublunaire* (1977), Viderman continued the illustration of his favourite topics by clinical examples and studies of Freud's writings, thereby showing that he too believed in the "return to Freud", language and metapsychology. He also stressed his concern for the subject's history in the treatment:

> The role I assign to the interplay of transference and counter-transference in no way detracts from the importance I attach to history—but a history made up only of events is not enough; the fantasies and myths constructed from the surviving parts of the history are necessary too. [Viderman, 1977, p. 334]

2) Michel Neyraut

In 1974 Michel Neyraut also published a controversial book on the transference, in which he asserts at the outset (cf. the outline given in the volume) that the countertransference takes precedence over the transference—in other words, that the countertransference is both temporally and logically prior to the transference within the dialectical field of the treatment. The precedence of analytic thought over the discovery of the transference is, he says, not only manifest in Freud but also exists in any analyst.

The transference, according to Neyraut, is actually a retroactive effect of Freud's discovery, appearing as an obstacle to an already constituted thought and technique; it therefore stands out against a context as a resistance. In order for a transference to exist, there must first be an analyst who tells a patient that he or she wishes to practise psychoanalysis on him or her. Next, the analyst must identify a repetition that concerns himself or herself in the patient's associations. The countertransference is thus defined as the involvement of the analyst anticipating the transference repetition and as an expected passion, which is on the one hand a technical error with respect to the attitude of pure observing neutrality, and on the other the grounds of the interpretation in the work of elucidating the transference. Instead of seeing the countertransference in limited terms as the reaction to the transference, Neyraut prefers the extensive theory that broadens the countertransference concept to include all the analyst's fantasies, ideas, feelings, interpretations and reactions, as long as the dynamic and conflictual link with the treatment is not lost sight of.

Neyraut goes on to distinguish two countertransference fields, which merge in practice. The external field has to do with the "date-stamped" character of goals, of the conception of the analysis, and of subordination to the implicit ideals of a given society, which operates insidiously. The internal field is the reaction of interest and seduction to the patient's words and transference. On the internal field, this author points out that during a session analytic thought is a resistance to the patient's process and transference, because it replaces action. Again, whereas interpretation proceeds from the manifest to the latent, thought goes the other way, from the latent to the manifest. The analyst is paid to suspend the course of his or her own thoughts and to surrender to someone else's associations. Neyraut agrees with Viderman that there is no such thing as neutral listening, or listening without identification with an object, whether of desire or of hate. The only solution for an analyst is to be capable of identifying and then of disidentifying. The worst configuration is when a resonance of character or structure arises between analyst and patient, resulting in an impasse.

As to the external field, Neyraut adduces the analyst's theory and writings:

> Any publication, writing or manifestation, although seemingly outside the analytic situation and its specific field, is in fact internal to the analyst ... Analytic thought gets up from its armchair and then returns to it ... If it feels the need to speak, to write, to develop the theory further, or even to demolish or transmit it, between these two sessions, it is because it cannot find enough in the analytic situation to satisfy it fully. [Neyraut, 1974, pp. 17–19, translated]

Finally, he mentions a gap in Freud's theory, the absence of a metapsychological formulation of the dialectical aspect of the analytic setting. According to Neyraut, this derives from Freud's relative ignorance of the role played by the object in psychic construction, as well as from a distrust of the countertransference. Without challenging Freud's second theory of the drives, he suggests that it tends to favour the notion of a strictly internal resistance—viscosity of the libido or death drive—as the explanation of negative therapeutic reaction, when it may in fact be the consequence of resistance towards the countertransference. He therefore calls for a new metapsychology: "If the transference and countertransference are seen as linked in the process, a transposition of metapsychology in the psychoanalytic situation becomes necessary" (1974, p. 69).

Neyraut offers some hints on the form this might take, to ensure that it does not block the therapeutic process, which is made up primarily of movement, symbolisation and the creation of something new. After all, if the transference and the countertransference are seen as interwoven in a dialectical field, this does not mean that they are being mixed up. One aspect is the intersection of affect and representation in the transference–countertransference field, in consequence of which the affect of one party encounters the representation of the other. This ensures that the unconscious-to-unconscious communication does not assume the psychotic form of a mirror confirmation, a divination or delusion à deux, that goes uncorrected by the analyst. Yet despite all the necessary efforts to

preserve the asymmetry of the transference and the countertransference, the former is not a pure repetition of the past, as
otherwise, in Neyraut's view, it would bring the process to a total
standstill: there is the reality of the countertransference, as a result
of which "the analyst is not the object of the transference but its
ultimate fantasy limit" (p. 219).

3) Piera Aulagnier

Aulagnier was one of the analysts who remained faithful to Lacan
after the first split, but who broke with him when his position became
more radical and formed the so-called Fourth Group (non-IPA). The
ideas presented in two books of hers that ensued from a series of
seminars held between 1973 and 1978—*La violence de l'interprétation*
and *Les destins du plaisir; aliénation, plaisir, passion*—seem to me to
resemble those of Viderman and Neyraut in certain respects.

For Aulagnier, the transference–countertransference asymmetry
is essential to the preservation of an analytic relationship, situation
and space. On the basis of the experience of the Lacanian
institutional upheavals and dramas of analytic training, she
demonstrates and criticises—even more severely than Viderman
with his idea of construction by the analyst—the possible alienation
of the patient by the arbitrary aspect of interpretations, which she
radically describes as the "violence of interpretation".

This violence, which, while of secondary importance in the
treatment, often goes unnoticed by the two partners, holds sway
over the subject by virtue of a power, a knowledge or an ideology. It
is favoured by the conditions of the therapy, especially where the
analytic situation is only an empty ritual, and by the antecedent of
primary violence in childhood, when the desire of the child's "I"
was enslaved to the pleasure of another, alienating, "I" by the vital
need of the child. For the infantile "I" has a vital need for a
spokesperson to formulate identity-related wishes on its behalf. The
risk here is that the countertransference might include a wish for
alienation of the patient on the level of passion owing to the
patient's transference love; this usually occurs when a residue of
passionate transference on to the training analyst remains from the
analyst's analysis, which has not been properly terminated with the
requisite mourning process.

4) Michel de M'Uzan

De M'Uzan is one of France's most original thinkers on the countertransference. His work on the countertransference and the paradoxical system dates back to 1976 and 1978 (*La bouche de l'inconscient* was published in the latter year), and is still ongoing.

His ideas originally flowed from a clinical observation of his own functioning in a session:

> While the analyst listens to his or her patient, there arise strange representations, a range of multi-coloured images, reveries and the like ... bearing no comprehensible relation to what is happening. One is tempted to say that the analyst has gone away, and that this is a manifestation of the countertransference in the strict sense. [de M'Uzan, 1976, p. 165, translated]

This does not mean that that the analyst's attention flags. Rather than seeming to fall asleep, the analyst experiences a floating sensation akin to a slight depersonalisation, or a sense of strangeness. Nor, in de M'Uzan's view, are these thoughts exactly the same as the affective resonance described by Paula Heimann in 1949, since they appear in the form of sentences—for instance, "I'd like to eat you up, you lovely sailor",[3] as a response to the patient's addressing him as "Monsieur" in an unusual way. If the analyst divulges these thoughts to the patient at the appropriate time, they may prove to anticipate an important juncture in the treatment.

Now these thoughts are not the fruit of subterranean work performed by the analyst on the patient's material along the lines described by Annie Reich. They are instead more in the nature of an obliteration of the boundaries of the analyst's ego, whereby the analyst's psychical apparatus can be put at the patient's disposal to operate in a paradoxical system in the form of a creation made up of two unconsciouses—a kind of chimera endowed with a life of its own, as de M'Uzan puts it.

Of course, this phenomenon presupposes the satisfaction of some special conditions. First, the analyst must be prepared to receive the patient in the depths of his or her being, in his or her internal "reception system"—what de M'Uzan calls "fundamental silence" or the "mouth of the unconscious". By virtue of his or her capacity for primary identification, the analyst will receive important fragments of the patient's unconscious. The process could be described as one of projective identification for the patient and introjective identification for the analyst, but de M'Uzan prefers Freudian to Kleinian formulations, finding the latter too mechanical. In his view, the process is more one of interpenetration, facilitated by the broadening of the analyst's "identity spectrum" and the permeability of the analyst's preconscious. The most harmful countertransference at this stage is rejection of the analysand like a foreign body or graft just when the regression of thought in the countertransference gives rise to quasi-paranoid experiences in the analyst. There may then be a flight into instinctual temptation (according to Greenson) or, alternatively, withdrawal, sometimes accompanied by falling asleep.

In a later paper, "Pendant la séance" (1989–91), de M'Uzan distinguishes the creation of a "chimera" from empathy and from the ordinary countertransference. The progress of his experience with difficult patients—together with Fain and Marty, he was one of the founders of the Paris Psychosomatic School—was based more on his work on the countertransference than on ideas about modification of the setting; the only parameter he developed was the notion of psychic reception by the analyst, facilitated by the analyst's tolerance of regression to the limits of aphanisis, which in his view was tantamount to the risk of total loss of the analyst's capacity to represent.

Having reached this level of regression, the analyst develops what de M'Uzan calls a "shield-antenna", whereby he or she can advance step by step, alternating between listening, regression and verbalising for the purpose of interpretation. Countertransference resistance is then at its peak and may assume three forms: (1) deposition (like a parasitic insect laying eggs in a host body) in the patient's psychical apparatus, signifying a wish to reverse the process of introjective identification; (2) covetousness, or intent to use the patient's material primarily for the analyst's self-analysis; (3) domination, in which the analyst seeks to exercise strict control over the patient's psychic functioning.

Finally, it is worth noting that, like other French analysts (Anzieu or Pontalis), de M'Uzan is also a writer when the spirit moves him. At a recent symposium, Dufour (1998) suggested that this might be a manifestation of a literary countertransference, in which the analyst uses writing as a "reception device" to express in narrative form analytic countertransference experiences that could not be represented other than by this roundabout route.

5) Joyce McDougall

This author's contribution to the "work of the countertransference" (Urtubey, 1994) is in some respects similar to de M'Uzan's. Like him, she adopts a simple style, based on her experience with cases at the limit of analysability. Like him, too, she performs a stimulating and exemplary function through her "pleas" for the analyst to be available to "anti-analysands"—subjects who have constructed "neo-sexualities" (she prefers this term to the pejorative word "perversions") or psychosomatic patients. In addition, she combines a constant concern to analyse her own countertransference with great flexibility in the handling of the setting (Janin-Oudinot, 2000).

Her paper "Countertransference and primitive communication" (1975) contains her theoretical contribution on the subject, in which she suggests that early, pre-verbal traumatic disturbances are not registered in the preconscious and are therefore not accessible to memory (as we have seen, Viderman shared this view). Patients who have had such experiences thus use their words as acts, to make the analyst feel what for them has no name—just as the mother was the child's apparatus for thinking thoughts. The analyst then feels the effects of this primitive communication; for example, McDougall reports that, on seeing that one of her female patients was in good spirits after a session that had left her feeling discouraged, she asked her whether she was supposed to shed the patient's tears on her behalf.

As in the case of a screaming child, the primitive communication evacuates fragments of primary affective experience in a funda-mental transference that seeks to abolish completely any difference between self and other. If the analyst accepts this, he or she goes back to a stage at which the child has one body for two and one psyche for two; this is another instance of the chimera, but with more emphasis on affect than in de M'Uzan. McDougall was to develop this idea further in *Theaters of the Mind* (1985; original French edition 1982) and *Theatres of the Body* (1989). The metaphor of the theatre is, as we have seen, a recurring element in French psychoanalysis, the analytic space being represented as the staging of the unconscious. This is one of the rare points of agreement between McDougall, Green and … Lacan!

In her latest book, *The Many Faces of Eros* (1996), McDougall continues her plea in favour of the neo-sexualities as creative solutions to the problem of psychic survival, while at the same time seeking to "put psychoanalysis on the couch"—that is, undertaking a serious analysis of the theoretical, ideological and institutional countertransferences to which analysts too often succumb. She points out that psychoanalysis differs from other sciences in that most of its theoretical concepts are not demonstrable, so that the sacralisation of concepts and the adulation (or execration) of their authors prove to be due to unresolved transferences in analysts and in disputes between analytic schools.

6) J.-B. Pontalis

Pontalis, a member of the French Psychoanalytical Association (formed after a second split in 1963, this time from the Lacan group, and later a component society of the IPA), is among those who have written most on the countertransference. This is presumably due to his particular sensibility, which soon caused him to break free of all dogmatic theoretical schools and to forge a personal style halfway between psychoanalysis and literature.

In "Le mort et le vif entrelacés" (1975), Pontalis comments ironically on the fashion of delighting in the display of one's countertransference, as if to say that one is seeing with one's blind spots, listening to what one is deaf to, and conscious of one's unconscious. Even if this is indeed a possible way of recognising the patient's unconscious conflict, there is nothing self-evident about it, and Pontalis draws particular attention to the case of patients with whom the analyst feels nothing, which is actually a manifestation of a countertransference that is still more difficult because disembodied. The very antithesis of patients whose pathology results from too explosive a primal scene, who introduce a noisy, destructive couple to the transference and the countertransference, these subjects are surely the children of mortified, starvation-bearing couples. Now the only genuine countertransference, worthy of the name, is in Pontalis's view not the countertransference that touches one to the quick but, conversely, that which mortifyingly touches the analyst "with death".

He now sketches out a scale of countertransferences, which he describes in detail in *La force d'attraction* (1990). The first level is the project, the analyst's analytic enterprise, which differs for each analyst and is therefore not susceptible to generalisation like Lacan's "desire of the analyst". The second level is that of surprise, evoked in an analyst who is "touched to the quick"—a psychic movement in resonance with a sensitive point in the analyst. The third level is the point where the countertransference "takes hold"—that is, the place permanently assigned to the analyst by the patient—and the less that place corresponds to the one the analyst assigns to himself or herself, the more likely the process is to come to a standstill. The fourth level is that of mastery[4]—the countertransference proper, which, for Pontalis, is the one that threatens the sanity or intellectual competence of the analyst or to terrify him or her.

Pontalis's latest book, *Fenêtres* (2000), written in an extremely literary style, includes several passages that as it were mesh directly with the countertransference. It is as if the analyst, feeling threatened in his mental functioning, were taking care of himself by dreaming, giving his memory free rein, and then turning the result into a work of literature, with a view to working through something that may have become frozen in him. But writing too can become fixed, just as interpretation can be over-hasty, if the analyst does not wait until he has assimilated the process sufficiently and substitutes his own theory for the patient's. In a highly condensed form reminiscent of jottings on a piece of paper, Pontalis presents the fruits of his reflections one by one: as an analyst, one should distrust the talons of the concept and the *idée fixe*; be fond of one's patients (but not too fond, as excess here would constitute destructive love); take care of oneself if one cannot detach oneself from patients' material; go to the window and question oneself; try to open up a clear path to one's memories; and look after one's working instrument—namely, oneself.

Pontalis's extra-analytic approach here seems to me to be quite close to that of such authors as de M'Uzan, or Anzieu in his analysis of Beckett (1992), which Anzieu sees as a way of continuing his self-analysis.

7) Jean-Luc Donnet

Donnet is one of the group of French psychoanalysts interested in the dynamic conflict between the setting and the analytic field (which he calls the "analytic site"). The starting point for his reflections was a book written jointly with Green, *L'Enfant de Ça* (Donnet & Green, 1973), in which the two authors consider theory as the retaliation of the countertransference following a failure, and discuss the triangular relationship arising between the patient, the analyst and the analyst's theory.

Green himself has written little on the countertransference, apart from a few notes in "The analyst, symbolization and absence in the analytic setting" (1974) and "Le silence du psychanalyste" (1979–82), where he stresses the analyst's role as the guardian of the setting. Green's theory has nevertheless been an essential element in the French understanding of the setting and the negative of the representation, which is, as we shall see, so important in the way the countertransference "takes hold".

Donnet therefore developed his ideas alone in "Contre-transfert, transfert sur l'analyse" (1976), where he points out that the countertransference was discovered in the interanalytic field, in discussions among analysts that allowed the protagonists to stand back from their experiences (he mentions Freud's "The future prospects of psycho-analytic psychotherapy" [1910]). This contribution dealt with supervisions and meetings between analysts. However, this realisation was supplemented by Ferenczi's insistence that the analyst should himself have undergone analysis, a demand accepted by Freud. In this way, what had been seen as countertransference towards a patient became a matter of the treatment of the analyst-to-be—of a "transference on to analysis". A tension may thus be discerned between the response to the patient's transference—which will be the subject of self-analysis of the analyst's nascent countertransference manifestations—and the analytic function defined by theory.

Patients sometimes compel the analyst to question the analytic setting, and in particular neutrality. In some cases a simple elaboration of the countertransference response is enough. Another vital point is whether the analyst gives priority to the analytic ideal or to the treatment of an individual patient; Winnicott espoused the second of these positions, saying that when he was unable to do analysis he would do something else. Finally, in this conception the setting is one of waiting—that is, the materialisation of the analyst's countertransference as transference on to analysis.

Later, in *Le divan bien tempéré* (1995), Donnet was to focus on the growing demand for an ideal of purity in analyst training, with the associated risk of ideologies of the setting (and hence of a countertransference that would be unresolvable in the theoretical setting). At first Freud had recommended self-analysis of dreams only. After this came the rule of analysis of the analyst, who gradually found himself or herself required to be "thoroughly analysed", and then to have regular periods of analysis, supervisions and so on. This demand for training is detrimental to the spontaneity of the transference in the analyst-to-be, who is likely to be less well analysed than his or her patients. The French solution of total separation of the analyst's analysis from training is a step forward here, but the ultimate, albeit undefined, aim of analysis of the analyst is, Donnet suggests, disidentification, and the de-idealisation of institutional objectives.

7) Jean Guillaumin

This author extends the idea of analysis of the countertransference and its setting. The setting, in his view, is not content merely to annex the walls of the stage, or even the wings, but overflows into events outside the theatre, in the street, as it were off the recognised field of play. His work on the countertransference dates back to 1987, but reached its full flowering in the nineteen nineties with his commentary on Urtubey's paper in 1994 and his 1998 book *Transfert, contre-transfert,* which recapitulates and supplements his previous contributions.

Guillaumin begins this book with a critique of the notion of the therapeutic alliance, which he connects with the Kleinians' reliance on the healthy part of the ego, Balint's consideration of the primary need for love and, also, Parat's "basic relationship" (1976). This is the notion of an invisible support the patient obtains from a real object, a support that does not call the object itself into question because it is inherent in the psychoanalytic setting. His criticisms are subtle, because for a long time he himself thought it necessary to respect a part of "the transference anaclitosis" (a term meaning support, attachment or an anaclitic link in borderlines) without looking at it too closely. Its counterpart is a "fundamental counter-transference", in which the analyst "sticks to the transference" and is prepared partially to rule out speech and the third element.

In Guillaumin's view, this resembles the "bottomless" counter-transference occurring in any analysis, and in particular that of an analyst-to-be; it is a countertransference of which a part is destined never to be elucidated, to remain in the shadow of the unsaid, of what the analyst has failed to notice, so that it cannot be included in his or her interpretive work. Eventually, however, Guillaumin's position changes: he comes to believe that the failure of many seemingly successful analyses is due to the neglect of this fundamental countertransference, often connected with persons known to both parties or common ideals or that go unanalysed precisely because they are shared.

Like others (Urtubey, 1994), Guillaumin draws attention to the difficulty presented by the countertransference with borderlines— patients with split egos. Splitting of the ego is more frequent than we think, and underlies the resistant portion of repression (the unrepresentable traumatic part, or primal repression). This split-off part gives rise to a split in the countertransference. As a part of this, an uncompleted familial mourning process, including denial of mourning, can be exported on to the analyst (a mechanism described by Racamier, one that differs from projective identifica-tion). To mitigate the split, consciousness and interpretation are not enough; an accidental breach of the setting is often also needed, to undo the transference–countertransference collusion that has become ensconced in it, as well as a commitment by the analyst to reintroduce affect.

Another particularity of such cases is that the analyst must take care, after what may be a very long period of time, to emerge from the dual relationship in which he or she follows the patient closely. The oedipal situation will not come about by itself if the analyst merely analyses containment, separation anxiety and dependence. Failure to discern the defensive function of pregenital, narcissistic and regressive material; constantly focusing the transference on oneself or seeing oneself as its only object; mixing up the father and mother imagos in the transference instead of distinguishing them—

these are the pitfalls of a countertransference that resists the patient's oedipal development and is likely to make an analysis interminable.

If the analyst-to-be internalises the model of the training analyst without modulation by mourning, supervisions and an adequate third-element role played by the institution, the countertransference may be turned back on his or her own person or it may overflow. Identification, which persists owing to the reality of transmission, reflects the non-completion of the analyst's analysis. But, Guillaumin then asks, what is the training analyst to transmit that will not prove to be a stumbling block in the analyst-to-be's countertransference with his or her patients?

A critique of Lacan's idea that love is giving something one does not have leads Guillaumin to conclude that what training analysts transmit is not what they have (their supposed knowledge), nor what they do not have (the lack, or de-being, in Lacan's terms, that underlies a masochistic ideology), but their capacity to endure not having, to contain their lack without annihilating it, and to tolerate frustration; this he calls the *part-en-tiers*.[5]

Finally, Guillaumin is one of the authors who have tried to accede to Neyraut's demand for a metapsychology of the transference–countertransference field, and even expresses surprise that so few have taken up the challenge—perhaps, he suggests, because of the endogamic, family aspect of the first groups of analysts. In his view, this field includes a central "canal zone" in the analyst's psychical apparatus that has remained "tender", whose professional brief is to facilitate intimate communication with the untamed, ill-contained and unelaborated aspects of the patient's psychical apparatus. This zone, which corresponds to de M'Uzan's chimera, is a trap for the negative, the unrepresented.

The interface between the two is at first fuzzy, and it is only in a second phase that it becomes possible to distinguish the relative contributions of the transference and the countertransference in the common field. This confusion is well represented by the couch–armchair configuration in the session, which Guillaumin sees as the coming together of two cephalic spaces, of two heads speaking with merged voices while the associated bodies remain distinct.

The canal zone thus defined is contained and protected by a framework of facilitating technical measures (the setting). Some "play" must exist between the setting and the strangeness of the intimate encounter; it is this intermediate space that constitutes the authenticity of analysis, as well as the aim of transmission where this is not confined to an identification with the analyst. However, work on groups and the psychoses has shown that some transference and countertransference phenomena are exported beyond the limits of the ego and of the analytic setting. Even if the seduction of the patient–analyst encounter and of the analytic configuration attracts many scattered cathexes, a portion of the old cathexes of patient and analyst alike will remain outside the setting, while another portion will attach itself to the "manifest" part of the setting. Hence there are invisible meeting places between patient and analyst, located in the hidden part of the setting, or even outside the setting—what Guillaumin calls the "hinterland of the setting". Examples are common acquaintances, shared ideals, or even complicity with whoever referred the patient. If unanalysed, these zones of complicity resist elaboration and oppose the dissolution of the transference–countertransference link (Guillaumin, 2000).

Outlook: other scenes

I must unfortunately end this paper without discussing the work of a number of authors who really deserve a place in it. These include Anzieu and C. & S. Botella for their contribution on the dynamic of the double in the analyst (1984); Chasseguet-Smirgel for the feminine aspect of the countertransference (1984); Cournut for the "mole" of the passionate countertransference (1990); Denis and his idea of the countertransference as a vicissitude of the transference (1988); Faimberg for "listening to [the patient's] listening" (1981, 1992); Fain for the "interpreter's wish" (1982); Fédida (1992), Lebovici (1994); Parat for the basic relationship (1976); Rouart (1976); Roussillon (1992, 1995) and Stein for what he calls the "reserved sector of the transference" (1977). As stated, I have confined my review to those analysts who have devoted a high proportion of their work to the countertransference, and the authors not discussed here conform to a greater or lesser extent to my chosen representative examples.

However, I should like to conclude by presenting some personal ideas, which I believe reflect the trend of French psychoanalysis in general rather than constituting a truly original position. They stem from countertransference work on my practice as a whole, as well as from ongoing reading and discussions, involving in particular the French authors already mentioned.

The countertransference is an essential component of the treatment; without it, one would only need to invent a psycho-analyst-computer on which to run an interactive programme representing the transference/countertransference field. However, a long road remains to be travelled to optimise the role and understanding of the countertransference. As shown above, the French analysts have made contributions on three of its aspects: (1) its part in the work of interpretation and historical construction of the subject in analysis, with the history of psychoanalysis and the analyst's technique and training as a counterpoint; (2) its ambiguous structure, in effect an extension of the ego's boundaries, which gives rise to the hybrid chimera of a psyche for two; and (3) the inclusion of the setting, as the guardian of the existence of a third entity (Green, 1989) to contain the regressive process and permit emergence from the dual relationship, although the setting has its blind spots and there is always the possibility of collusion outside the setting.

The work of the countertransference, as understood by Urtubey—i.e. work based on the analyst's listening and presence, culminating in interpretation—can to my mind be facilitated by observance of the following principles.

1) *A diversity principle.* This concerns the need to avoid fixing the countertransference in a repetitive posture. Success here is most likely if the analyst does everything possible to preserve the essential diversity of the transference registers, interpretive styles and theories underlying the technique he uses with the patient over time.

2) *A principle of psychic life.* The value of the countertransference, where the analyst can elaborate it and work it into the theatre of the treatment, is that it can help the patient to achieve a better representational life that will include affect, the imaginary and language, albeit sometimes at the cost of dramas or acting out.

3) *A principle of temporality and history.* This is necessary to allow a private psychic space to succeed the ambiguous space of the field, and the patient's identification and the "adhesion" of the countertransference to give way to disidentification and interpretive detachment—for one of the aims of the analytic process is to help the subject make sense of his or her life and history.

On the basis of these reference points and the view of the psychic space taken from Viderman and others, I shall now describe the various loci and aspects of the countertransference, from the centre outwards.

1) In the centre, the analyst's response to the direct transference—on to his or her "psychic body"—is variable; the analyst sometimes has difficulty in accepting the encounter with the formless and the unknown "without memory or desire" (as recommended by Bion). In the case of a fragment of traumatic experience that has undergone little elaboration by representation, symbolisation and the binding forces of libido, the traumatic effect in the countertransference is substantial, although the impact depends on the sensitivity of the target: a mirror resonance or cumulative trauma may have formidable effects on an analyst's psychic life, and perhaps even stop him or her from being an analyst temporarily or permanently.

At this level, what determines the receptive capacity of the analyst is the depth of the regression attained in his or her own analysis, coupled with the analyst's ability to emerge from and mourn for it without excessive residues. As de M'Uzan has shown, the capacity to endure the constitution of a chimera *à deux* depends on the analyst's being able to tolerate a degree of depersonalisation. The analyst must be capable of bearing the "madness of the countertransference"—as it were, primary maternal madness. I have attempted various descriptions of this state as experienced in the treatment of very disturbed patients: theoretical delusion (Duparc, 1987), confusion of identity (Duparc, 1991), or a negative hallucination in the countertransference (Duparc, 1996).

2) Where the patient brings relatively well elaborated traces, imagos or roles assigned by the transference can be identified. The analyst may be prepared to assume these roles, and take

more or less pleasure in so doing. As Urtubey has shown, the various theories of the countertransference give priority to particular kinds of roles: there are theories of domination (paternal), totalist theories (maternal), theories of self-analysis of the countertransference (infantile), and theories of the analytic couple. In themselves, these theories are—especially if the analyst believes in them somewhat too strongly—"freeze-frame images" of the countertransference (Duparc, 1994a). In my view, the diversity principle requires the analyst never to cast himself in a single role for too long.

The analyst must therefore adopt different roles in the counter-transference and not remain rigidly in a single one of them for any length of time. These may be: (a) the role of the father, who offers distancing and helps one to master and obey the rules, on pain of the threat of (protective) castration; (b) the role of the under-standing mother who takes in the patient's unverbalisable affective reactions and translates them for the patient—but this mother must also be capable of becoming a woman and a love partner again, and of allowing the patient to become autonomous; (c) the role of the child excluded from the primal scene—of the abandoned child that must muddle through by itself and look after its parents if it is to be able to survive; (d) the role of love partner within the couple—of father or mother, of lover or mistress, on the sexual level and on that of tenderness and complicity; and (e) the role of the double, brother or twin, of friend and confidant, or other self; although seldom mentioned, this role is sometimes important (cf. Botella & Botella, 1984).

3) However, patients on occasion need to bring areas of their history or experience that cannot be represented because they persist only in the form of perceptual or traumatic traces, of aspects of behaviour unrepresentable in words, dreams or images. The analyst can admittedly take these into himself or herself in the countertransference, elaborating them into a form in which they can be "dreamed", hallucinated and then verbalised for the patient. Often, though, they are too traumatic for the analyst to bear in the direct transference, so that he or she negatively hallucinates them (Duparc, 1996), while the patient deposits them on the walls of the analytic setting. In this way the patient may attack a particular aspect of the concrete setting, or

cathect it in a concealed way that is invisible to the analyst—e.g. the couch, payment, the place of the analysis, or a given object in the setting—and the invisible negative transference on to the setting will be revealed only in the event of a discontinuity in this cathexis (for instance, if something is missing or changes). The analyst must also be able to reintroduce this cathexis, which spares him or her in the transference on to the analyst's person. This will be even harder in the case of something the analyst sees as normal and justified, such as the technical parameters of the treatment—benevolence, neutrality, the analyst's silence, the patient's free associating, transference interpretations, and so on. I showed in a contribution on the technical parameters of the setting (Duparc, 1994b, 1995) how each of these parameters could become an ideology in the service of one of the five primal fantasies that make up the Oedipus complex (castration, seduction, return to the mother's womb, cannibalistic incorporation and the primal scene). If these parameters come to resonate, however faintly, with the patient's structure, the result will be a countertransference blinding that may well become permanent unless the analyst is prepared to review his or her setting and interpretive strategy periodically. As Donnet (1995) saw, ideologies belonging to the training analyst or to the analytic institution form part of the setting and constitute its outside wall, even if this is often hidden by the more conspicuous classical transference–countertransference interaction.

The components of this "countertransference on to the setting" include the analyst's theory and training, which may or may not make for a degree of flexibility in the rhythm and length of sessions and the rhythm of interpretations, thus allowing a secure rhythm à deux to arise. Some rigid schools seize upon an ideological parameter, such as cutting off and castration for Lacanians who favour short sessions, regression in the lap of the maternal countertransference for the Kleinian advocates of long, frequent sessions, and so on (Duparc, 1990, 1997).

4) An even more worrying form is the lateral countertransference, whereby the analyst neglects a part of the transference which cannot address itself to the analyst and which instead chooses a partner outside the treatment or is directed to an event or extra-analytic project for the purpose of resistance. The analyst can

readily become aware of such situations if they involve a member of the patient's family (a spouse, parent or child), although there may be a temptation not to devote sufficient attention to what goes on outside the treatment if the analyst would rather not see certain aggressive, perverse or regressive manifestations as directed towards himself or herself.

Yet aspects of behaviour, too, may constitute split-off areas that the analyst may easily overlook because not represented by dreams or associations. They include addictive behaviour, actions leading to psychosomatic pathology, or sexual habits (Ferenczi). The countertransference is then relegated to a mere counter-attitude, and the only course remaining open to the patient may be to break off the treatment and resume it again after a period of latency in the hope that the analyst will meanwhile have succeeded in becoming aware of the situation and overcoming it.

Notes

1. [In English in the original.]
2. "Matheme" is a neologism coined by Lacan to refer to the relationship between several symbols of a mathematical nature, which is supposed to represent a structure in the unconscious.
3. There is a sexual undertone here. Moreover, the strangeness is due to the fact that the person concerned is a woman, not a man, and to the similarity with the style of a French popular song.
4. In the sense of Freud's *Bemächtigung*.
5. Guillaumin's term for the part that belongs to the third element or party—a part of the dual identification that is cut off and reserved for the third party in the oedipal constellation; the word *en* connotes the place of the third element or party in transmission.

References

Anzieu, D. (1992). *Beckett et le Psychanalyste*. Paris: Mentha-Archimbaud.
Aulagnier, P. (1975). *La Violence de l'Interprétation*. Paris: Presses Univ. France.
Aulagnier, P. (1979). *Les Destins du Plaisir*. Paris: Presses Univ. France.
Bleger, J. (1967). Psicoanálisis del encuadre psicoanalítico. *Rev. Psicoanál.*, 24: 241–258.

Botella, C. & Botella, S. (1984). L'homosexualité inconsciente et la dynamique du double en séance. *Rev. franç. psychanal.*, *48*: 687–708.

Bouvet, M. (1956–57). Transfert, contre-transfert et réalité. Les variations de la technique, distance et variations. In: *La Relation d'Objet* (pp. 227–293). Paris: Payot, 1985.

Chasseguet-Smirgel, J. (1984). The femininity of the analyst in professional practice. *Int. J. Psychoanal.*, *65*: 169–178.

Cournut, J. (1990). La taupe ou le cas difficile d'un contre-transfert passionnel. *Rev. franç. psychanal.*, *54*: 329–343.

Denis, P. (1988). L'avenir d'une désillusion: le contre-transfert, destin du transfert. *Rev. franç. psychanal.*, *52*: 829–840.

Donnet, J.-L. (1976). Contre-transfert, transfert sur l'analyse. Analyse définie et indéfinissable. In: *Le Divan Bien Tempéré*. Paris: Presses Univ. France, 1995.

Donnet, J.-L. & Green, A. (1973). *L'Enfant de Ça*. Paris: Minuit.

Donnet, J.-L. (1995). *Le Divan Bien Tempéré*. Paris: Presses Univ. France, 1995.

Dufour, J. (1998). Le sourire de l'avocat, un contre-transfert littéraire? In: F. Duparc (Ed.), *L'Art du Psychanalyste*. Lausanne: Delachaux & Niestlé.

Duparc, F. (1987). Le regard comme étayage (cadre et cadrage en psychanalyse) [foreword by A. Green]. In: *L'Élaboration en Psychanalyse*. Bordeaux-Paris: Presses Univ. France, L'Esprit du Temps, 1998.

Duparc, F. (1990). Du bon usage des métaphores théoriques (Reich, Lacan, Bion). *Rev. franç. psychanal.*, *55*: 233–46.

Duparc, F. (1991). Sujet à confusion. *Rev. franç. psychanal.*, *55*: 1237–1251.

Duparc, F. (1994a). Arrêt sur image dans le contre-transfert. *Rev. franç. psychanal.*, *58*: 1691–1700.

Duparc, F. (1994b). Tout analyser? Les paramètres idéologiques de la cure [foreword by A. Green]. In: *L'Élaboration en Psychanalyse*. Bordeaux-Paris: Presses Univ. France, L'Esprit du Temps, 1998.

Duparc, F. (1995). *L'Image du Psychanalyste*. Paris: L'Harmattan.

Duparc, F. (1996). Lorsque l'analyste s'absente de lui-même; hallucination négative dans le contre-transfert [foreword by A. Green]. In: *L'Élaboration en Psychanalyse*. Bordeaux-Paris: Presses Univ. France, L'esprit du temps, 1998.

Duparc, F. (1997). Le temps en psychanalyse. Rapport du congrès de Paris. *Rev. franç. psychanal.*, *61*: 1429–1488.

Fain, M. (1982). *Le Désir de l'Interprète*. Paris: Aubier-Montaigne.

Faimberg, H. (1981). Une difficulté de l'analyse: la reconnaissance de l'altérité (l'écoute de l'interprétation). *Rev. franç. psychanal.*, 45: 1351–1367.

Faimberg, H. (1992). The countertransference position and the counter-transference. *Int. J. Psychoanal.*, 73: 541–546.

Fédida, P. (1992). *Crise et Contre-transfert.* Paris: Presses Univ. France.

Freud, S. (1910). The future prospects of psycho-analytic psychotherapy. *S.E., 11.*

Freud, S. (1941). Findings, ideas, problems. *S.E., 23.*

Green, A. (1974). L'analyste, la symbolisation et l'absence. In: *La Folie Privée.* Paris: Gallimard, 1990. [English: The analyst, symbolization and absence in the analytic setting. *Int. J. Psychoanal.*, 56: 1–22, 1975.]

Green, A. (1977). La royauté appartient à l'enfant (sur D. Winnicott). *L'arc, 69:* 4–12.

Green, A. (1979–1982). Le silence du psychanalyste. In: *La Folie Privée.* Paris: Gallimard, 1990.

Green, A. (1989). Du tiers; de la tiercéïté. In: *La Psychanalyse, Questions pour Demain, Monographies de la Rev. franç. Psychanal.* (pp. 243–279). Paris: Presses Univ. France, 1990.

Guillaumin, J. (1998). *Transfert, Contre-transfert.* Bordeaux-Paris: Presses Univ. France, L'esprit du temps.

Guillaumin, J. (2000). *L'Invention de la Pulsion de Mort.* Paris: Dunod.

Janin-Oudinot, M. (2000). Le théâtre du contre-transfert. In: F. Duparc (Ed.), *Joyce McDougall aux 1001 Visages.* Lausanne: Delachaux & Niestlé.

Lacan, J. (1951). Intervention sur le transfert. In: *Écrits* (pp. 215–226). Paris: Seuil, 1966.

Lacan, J. (1953). Fonction et champ de la parole et du langage en analyse. In: *Écrits* (pp. 237–322). Paris: Seuil, 1966.

Lacan, J. (1960). *L'Éthique de la Psychanalyse, Séminaire no. 7.* Paris: Seuil. [English: D. Porter (Trans.), *The Seminar of Jacques Lacan, Book VII.* New York: Norton, 1992.]

Lacan, J. (1977). *Écrits* [English edition]. London: Hogarth.

Lebovici, S. (1994). Empathie et 'enactment' dans le travail de contre-transfert. *Rev. franç. psychanal.*, 58: 1550–1551.

Leon de Bernardi, B. (2000). The countertransference: a Latin American view. *Int. J. Psychoanal.*, 81: 331–351.

McDougall, J. (1975). Le contre-transfert et la communication primitive. In: *Plaidoyer pour une Certaine Anormalité.* Paris: Gallimard, 1978. [English: 'Countertransference and primitive communication'. In:

Plea for a Measure of Abnormality (pp. 247–298). New York: Int. Univ. Press, 1980.]

McDougall, J. (1982). *Théâtres du Je*. Paris: Gallimard. [English: *Theaters of the Mind. Illusion and Truth on the Psychoanalytic Stage*. New York: Basic Books.]

McDougall, J. (1989). *Théâtres du Corps*. Paris: Gallimard. [English: *Theatres of the Body*. London: Free Association.]

McDougall, J. (1996). *Éros aux Mille et un Visages*. Paris: Gallimard. [English: *The Many Faces of Eros. A Psychoanalytic Exploration of Human Sexuality*. New York: Norton, 1995.]

M'Uzan, M. de (1976). Contre-transfert et système paradoxal. In: *De l'Art à la Mort*. Paris: Gallimard, 1977.

M'Uzan, M. de (1978). La bouche de l'inconscient. In: *La Bouche de l'Inconscient*. Paris: Gallimard, 1994.

M'Uzan, M. de (1989–91). Pendant la séance. Du dérangement au changement. In: *La Bouche de l'Inconscient*. Paris: Gallimard, 1994.

Nacht, S. (1962). Le contre-transfert et les résistances. *Rev. franç. psychanal.*, 27: 133–138.

Nacht, S. (1963). *La Présence du Psychanalyste*. Paris: Presses Univ. France.

Neyraut, M. (1974). *Le Transfert*. Paris: Presses Univ. France, Le Fil Rouge.

Parat, C. (1976). A propos du contre-transfert. *Rev. franç. psychanal.*, 40: 545–560.

Pontalis, J.-B. (1975). À partir du contre-transfert. Le mort et le vif entrelacés. *Nouv. Rev. Psychanal.*, 12: 73–88.

Pontalis, J.-B. (1990). *La Force d'Attraction*. Paris: Seuil.

Pontalis, J.-B. (2000). *Fenêtres*. Paris: Gallimard.

Rouart, J. (1976). Contre-transfert et séduction. *Rev. franç. psychanal.*, 40: 413–442.

Roussillon, R. (1992). *Du Baquet de Mesmer au Baquet de Sigmund Freud. Une Archéologie du Cadre*. Paris: Presses Univ. France.

Roussillon, R. (1995). *Logiques et Archéologiques du Cadre Psychanalytique*. Paris: Presses Univ. France.

Stein, C. (1977). Le secteur réservé du transfert. In: *La Mort d'Œdipe*. Paris: Denoël.

Urtubey, L. de (1994). Le travail du contre-transfert. *Rev. franç. psychanal.*, 58: 1271–1272.

Viderman, S. (1968). Genèse du transfert et structure du champ psychanalytique. *Rev. franç. psychanal.*, 40: 1011–1024.

Viderman, S. (1970). *La Construction de l'Espace Analytique*. Paris: Denoël.

Viderman, S. (1974). La bouteille à la mer. *Rev. franç. psychanal.*, 46: 323–384.

Viderman, S. (1977). *Le Céleste et le Sublunaire*. Paris: Presses Univ. France, Le Fil Rouge.